100 Ways

To Grow A
Thriving Law Practice

Business Development Strategies For Law Firms
Whether Sole Practitioner or AmLaw 100

Library of Congress Cataloging-in-Publication Data

Keller, David King
100 Ways To Grow A Thriving Law Practice / David King Keller
    p. cm.
Includes index.
ISBN- 9781463517496
1. Law Firms– Marketing. 2. Lawyers-Marketing. 3. Law Practice - Business
Development. 4. Law Practice-Skill Level Rating I. Title

KF300.F66 2009
340'.0683--dc22

                                                    2009008218
2 3 4 5 6 7 8 9 10 11 12 13 14

Publisher: Business Books Publishing
145 Corte Madera Center, #520
Corte Madera, CA 94925

www.BusinessBooksPublishing.com

Discounts are available for books ordered in bulk. Special consideration is
given to state bars, CLE programs, and other bar-related organizations. Spiral
bound versions for easy fold over use are available. Inquire at: Business Books
Publishing, info@BusinessBooksPublishing.com, Fax: (415) 289-0566.

For information on business development sales and marketing consulting,
training, Executive Coaching, speaking engagements, audiotapes, videotapes
or other works by David King Keller contact Keller Business Development
Group at: info@ KellerBusinessDevelopmentGroup.com

Dedication

To my partner and wife,
Carmen Maria Keller,
without whom this book would
never have been accomplished.

To lawyers and those that support them.
When you're good, and when you're great,
you make the world better for all of us.
Thank you.

Letting people know how
you can help them,
that's marketing.

Securing a contract
from people to
compensate you for
helping them,
that's sales.

Table of Contents

A wise person is always open to new wisdom.

- Ancient Tree

Introduction

100 Ways To Grow A Thriving Law Practice is comprehensively designed to grow law firm revenue by providing practical, cost-effective and measurable marketing and business development strategies.

Over twenty years of marketing, advertising, public relations, sales and business development are summarized in easy to understand action steps.

The business growth ideas in ***100 Ways To Grow A Thriving Law Practice*** are intended to benefit firms of all sizes, from the sole practitioner to large established international law firms. Small to medium size firms use this book like an in-house marketing consultant. The Chief Marketing Officer (CMO), Chairman, Managing Partner (MP) and Practice Group Leader (PGL) of larger firms can provide this book to Associates and Partners as an idea generator to bring back to the Chairman, CMO, MP or PGL for review, comment and appropriate action.

Don't make the mistake and think this is 100 ways to grow every practice. These are 100 ways to grow a practice. The reader is just looking for those three to eighteen *Ways* that make sense for your specific firm and can make the six, seven or eight figure difference in net revenue growth.

If a small to medium sized firm only employs *Way #17, the Gold Mine Interviews*, a significant revenue opportunity worth five to seven figures should become readily apparent.

100 Ways focuses on specific actions that are designed to lead to business engagement agreements.

Your first step with *100 Ways* is to take the short Business Development Quiz. Then, quickly scan the 100 "Ways" for the ones that stand out and capture your imagination and give you a gut feeling that says, "This one has return-on-investment and the sweet smell of success written all over it." Many will only have time to review one or two *Ways* a day, that's fine.

For a particular idea one reader may say, "We've been doing that for years." For the same idea others will say, "We should have been doing that for years."

Avoid the error of being put off by the "silly" or "obvious." Any "silly" idea is capable of stimulating an off-shoot idea that generates very serious revenue. Some of the *Ways* may be "obvious," but are you doing the obvious?

Some *Ways* may appear similar. An important few are restated with slightly different wording for emphasis and action, while others have a slight but significant difference.

After each *Way* there is a little writing space for you to make a few quick notes as they occur to you in the moment. This is your book. Mark it up liberally.

Following the *Ways* list you will find Executive Coaching ROI, a Practice Area Rating Grid, The Art and Science of Selling, Business Development Action Sheets, an Expanded Business Development Quiz, and About The Author. For one to one coaching go to www.kbdag.com.

Business development consciousness is an ongoing pursuit for everyone in the firm, without exception. "When do you stop actively marketing?" The answer is, "When you retire." And if you want retirement to be on your schedule and at your preferred level of income, then go to the next page and take the Business Development Quiz.

Business Development Quiz

Self-examination is critical. If you don't know where you are, you won't know where you're going, or how to get there.

Each Quiz question suggests a business development and marketing opportunity. So, the Quiz is both an assessment tool and an idea generator.

Make liberal notes as key business growth ideas occur to you with every question. The word "firm" is used for practices of every size.

We can all name a major law practice that had been around for decades and decades and one day simply folded. Why? When the big sustaining clients and cases went away they simply had no back-up business "in the pipe." Why? They had not taken the day-to-day actions, like those in this book, to grow the business. And they hadn't done an honest assessment in time to make a difference.

Business Development Activities Rating Table

Rate each area from 0, the lowest, to a maximum of 10.

Item #	Research	Rate 0-10
1	Practice areas. Does the firm have a list of every possible practice area offered by the firm easily available for external consumption? Notes / Comments / Action Items:	

2	Internally, has the firm rated each practice area by the level of expertise in that area? (See Practice Area Rating Grid section of book.) Notes / Comments / Action Items:	
3	Revenue. Most revenue comes from which Top 5 practice areas? Do they break out the same when you compare gross to net? Notes / Comments / Action Items:	
4	Money. Does the firm know top 5 sources of past revenue in terms of client types? Notes / Comments / Action Items:	
5	Money. Has the firm clearly identified the source(s) of steady cash flow: what, where, who, when? Notes / Comments / Action Items:	
6	Money. Has the firm identified the sources of the big revenue gains, e.g. what, where, who, when? Notes / Comments / Action Items:	
7	Has the firm constructed a description of ideal clients within each key practice area? Notes / Comments / Action Items:	

8	Does the firm have a list of best ways to communicate with each practice area's target audience? Notes / Comments / Action Items:	
9	Ideas. Has each person in the firm (everyone without exception) turned in a list of 10 ideas to develop business for the firm? Notes / Comments / Action Items:	
10	Markets. Has the firm made a list of at least 500 companies, people, and groups that could hire the firm? And then prioritized by most preferred? Notes / Comments / Action Items:	
11	Does the firm have a written record on how each client heard about the firm and made the decision to go with the firm? Notes / Comments / Action Items:	
12	Has the firm reviewed the LexisNexis atVantage prospecting tool? Or has firm hired a business development consultant who has? Notes / Comments / Action Items:	

13	Marketing. Has the firm interviewed at least four law firm marketing companies? Notes / Comments / Action Items:	
14	Advertising. Has the firm interviewed at least 4 law firm advertising companies? Notes / Comments / Action Items:	
15	PR. Has the firm interviewed at least 4 law firm public relations companies? Notes / Comments / Action Items:	
16	Events. Has the firm interviewed 4 local event planners for promo ideas? Notes / Comments / Action Items:	
17	Google and Bing the firm name. How high up on the results does the firm name appear? Notes / Comments / Action Items:	

18	Hire. Has the firm hired or at least interviewed the business development consultant used by another successful firm? Notes / Comments / Action Items:	
19	NLP. Is each of our attorneys familiar with the fundamental science of rapport building as established by neurolinguistic programming (NLP) research? Notes / Comments / Action Items:	
20	Does firm have a Legal Marketing Director? Does that person belong to the LMA, Legal Marketing Association? Notes / Comments / Action Items:	
21	BizDev. Does the firm have monthly business development meetings assisted by or led by a business development professional? Notes / Comments / Action Items:	

Item #	Internet	Rate 0 to 10
1	Is each attorney registered on LinkedIn, FaceBook, and Twitter? Notes / Comments / Action Items:	
2	What is the firm's SEO, Search Engine Optimization, rating on Google and Bing? How many total listings? Notes / Comments / Action Items:	
3	What is the SEO of each member of the firm by name on Google and Bing? Notes / Comments / Action Items:	
4	When we Google and Bing a specific law practice area in the City how high is the firm listed? Example: intellectual property law, San Francisco. What is the firm's rating for each and every practice area in the geo area the firm serves? Does the firm know how to improve those listings? See book Index on Search Engine Optimization. Notes / Comments / Action Items:	

5	How would I rate the firm's e-commerce awareness?Does the firm have an in-house e-commerce expert, or has the firm consulted with a business development sub-contractor who can guide us in e-commerce? Notes / Comments / Action Items:	
6	Does the firm have an e-letter that goes out monthly? Increase points for weekly. Reduce points for quarterly, or annually. Notes / Comments / Action Items:	
7	Does the firm have at least one law lecture on YouTube? Notes / Comments / Action Items:	
8	Are there individual and community resources on firm's Website that drive clients and not-yet-clients to the site? Example: Local Charitable Events Calendar, Ten Questions You Must Ask When Approaching a Will, etc. See Index. Notes / Comments / Action Items:	

Item #	Network	Rate 0 to 10
1	Does the firm's network as if the business' existence depends on it? Notes / Comments / Action Items:	
2	How many conferences with prospective clients are firm members attending this year? Notes / Comments / Action Items:	
3	How many firm members are on Bar association committees? Which ones? Notes / Comments / Action Items:	
4	How many community orgs and non-profits have firm members on their boards? Which ones? Notes / Comments / Action Items:	
5	Politicians. How many politicians have a firm member as an advisor? How many Mayors, and City Council members have firm members advising them? Which ones? Notes / Comments / Action Items:	

6	Seasoned lawyers. How many seasoned lawyers are taken to lunch by firm members every month for business development advice and contacts? Notes / Comments / Action Items:	
7	Triple R. How many "reciprocal referral relationships" does the firm have? See Index. Notes / Comments / Action Items:	
8	Alumni. How many law school and other alumni events have firm members attended in past 12 months? Notes / Comments / Action Items:	
9	Clubs. Do firm members belong to the required clubs to maximize potential client contact? Notes / Comments / Action Items:	
10	Clients. When was the last time the firm informed a client (past or present) that the firm has "some excess capacity" that can accommodate a few new clients? Notes / Comments / Action Items:	

11	Politicians. When was the last time the firm took a politician to lunch? Notes / Comments / Action Items:	
12	Are the words "free" and "no charge" always included in the first sentence or two when discussing that first consult with a prospective client? Is the firm up to date on communication techniques based on the last three decades of advanced neurolinguistic science research? Notes / Comments / Action Items:	
13	Are the words "free" and "no charge" always included in the first sentence or two when discussing that first consult with a prospective client? Is the firm up to date on communication techniques based on the last three decades of advanced neurolinguistic science research? Notes / Comments / Action Items:	

Item #	**Marketing** Public Awareness, Advertising, Public Relations, Press, Media Relations	Rate 0 to 10
1	Does the firm have a full time Marketing Director called Chief Marketing Officer, CMO? Notes / Comments / Action Items:	
2	Does the firm have a part time Business Development Consultant / Coach versed in sales and marketing supporting the CMO? Or does the firm have a part time Business Development Consultant until business growth allows for hiring a CMO? Notes / Comments / Action Items:	
3	Is there a legal treatise on the firm's website that will come up on Google and Bing? Notes / Comments / Action Items:	
4	Is there anything on firm's website that will attract a website visitor besides basic firm information? Notes / Comments / Action Items:	

5	When someone does come to the firm do they receive something free that has firm contact details on it? Notes / Comments / Action Items:	
6	Press. How many press and media contacts does the firm have? How many for each outlet: magazines, newspaper, radio, and TV? At industry events do firm members seek out the media reps who are present, introduce themselves, and get their card? And do firm members ask the media rep what type of news items they are seeking? Notes / Comments / Action Items:	
7	Public speaking. How many public speaking engagements will firm participate in this year? Notes / Comments / Action Items:	
8	Has any firm member published a legal book? (See Index for reference to quickly and easily self publish.) Notes / Comments / Action Items:	

9	Are all key media outlets aware of the firm as a possible source for comment on certain subjects? Notes / Comments / Action Items:	
10	Is the firm going to LMA, Legal Marketing Association, seminars and events? Notes / Comments / Action Items:	
11	E-zines and e-newsletters. Does the firm have a weekly or monthly e-letter that goes out to an ever increasing mailing list? Notes / Comments / Action Items:	
12	Media. How often does the firm take a legal writer, editor, or publisher to lunch? Notes / Comments / Action Items:	
13	How many articles have been published by the firm members in the last 24 months? Notes / Comments / Action Items:	

14	Marketing. Has firm asked each member to submit at least 10 marketing ideas? Notes / Comments / Action Items:	
15	Has firm participated in a charitable function in the last 9 months that availed firm members of an audience greater than 100 people? Notes / Comments / Action Items:	
16	How would you rate current method of marketing the firm? Rate the firm's marketing as compared to other firms in your sphere of practice. Rate law firm members' alignment and support of firm's marketing objectives. Notes / Comments / Action Items:	

◇◇

Item #	**Goodwill** Public Awareness	Rate 0 to 10
1	Has firm participated in a charitable function in the last 6 months that availed firm members of an audience greater than 100 people? Notes / Comments / Action Items:	

2	Charities coming to you. Has the firm considered the website-visit-client-conversion-ratio and enormous ongoing goodwill with wealthy 501C3 board members by placing a "Charitable Events Calendar" link on firm's website? See Index for Charitable Events Calendar biz dev info page. Notes / Comments / Action Items:	
3	Does the firm get prospects to walk into its lobby for reasons other than pressing legal matters? Has the firm done the math on opening its conference room and hosting the occasional non-profit board meeting? Is firm aware of the basic laws of familiarity and choice? Notes / Comments / Action Items:	

◇◇◇◇◇◇◇◇◇◇◇◇◇◇◇◇◇◇◇◇◇◇◇◇◇◇◇◇◇◇◇◇◇◇◇◇◇◇◇

Item #	**Administration** Operations	Rate 0 to 10
1	Does the firm have a marketing director, or a business sales and marketing consultant? Notes / Comments / Action Items:	

2	Does the firm have a business development action list? With due dates? Notes / Comments / Action Items:	
3	Does every member of the firm have a business development plan? Do they look at it daily / weekly? Notes / Comments / Action Items:	
4	Does every member of the firm have a legal business development coach they can call confidentially at any time? Notes / Comments / Action Items:	

◇◇

Item #	**Image:** Culture, Reputation	Rate 0 to 10
1	Does the firm have a policy that 99% of all calls and emails receive some form of response on the same day? Notes / Comments / Action Items:	

2	Does the firm have a culture of always looking for and congratulating a job well done? Notes / Comments / Action Items:	
3	Firm Culture. Does firm have a "can do" culture? Notes / Comments / Action Items:	
4	Does the firm inculcate "everyone, everyone, everyone is a possible source of business, or business referral"? Does the firm send out the occasional memo reminding everyone in the firm that their next conversation with the mailman or hairdresser could bring in "the next big one"? Notes / Comments / Action Items:	

◇◇

Item #	**Legal World Presence**	Rate 0 to 10
1	Any firm member(s) on an ABA committee? Notes / Comments / Action Items:	

2	Are firm members active in their Law School alumni? Notes / Comments / Action Items:	
3	How many of the firm's cases are cited in legal reference publications? Notes / Comments / Action Items:	
4	How many in the firm are Law School faculty or lecturer? Notes / Comments / Action Items:	
5	How many other law firms send us business? Notes / Comments / Action Items:	
6	Is the firm respected as a Top 10 in one or more fields? Notes / Comments / Action Items:	
7	Do some media consider the firm as the "go to" source for certain legal topics? Notes / Comments / Action Items:	

Item #	Business Development Professionals	Rate 0 to 10
1	Does the firm know the difference between an outside PR or advertising firm and a trained law firm business development coach who works with individual firm members? Notes / Comments / Action Items:	
2	Does the firm regularly utilize a professional law practice business development consultant-trainer-coach? Notes / Comments / Action Items:	
3	Are there any members of the firm who could use a little executive level business development coaching support (focus) sensitively mixed in with their busy schedule by a seasoned coach who knows the value of every second? Notes / Comments / Action Items:	

For more Business Development Quiz questions go to the **Expanded Business Development Quiz** section in the back of the book.

Make use of time, let not advantage slip.

- William Shakespeare

100 Ways To Grow A Thriving Law Practice

1.1   Take a retired judge to lunch.

They're safe. They don't bite (anymore). And there's no potential conflict. And, wow, do they ever have the contacts!

Every practice area ends up in court at some point, some more than others. After ten plus years on the bench Judges will typically know about your client base or know people who know about your client base.

Introduce yourself. Give the judge a frame of reference, e.g. you might say, "My name is ___ and I'm a member of the local bar and I thought I might call you and invite you to lunch or breakfast. My purpose is to be a better attorney, and I hoped I might learn something from your experience. Maybe you could share something of your experience as a judge, and maybe how you came to choose the bench versus private practice. I'm sure anything we discuss will be of interest. Is there a favorite restaurant you like? My treat, of course."

Make it the restaurant of their choice and offer to pick them up or send a driver. Make lunch about them; their climb to the bench; their incredible contributions and critical decisions; and their heart-warming and heart wrenching stories. Are there any causes they are currently supporting? They just might open up and share some of their lifelong bits of knowledge and contacts.

Notes / Comments / Action Items:

I recommend you take care of the minutes and the hours will take care of themselves.

- Earl of Chesterfield

1.2   Take a retired judge to lunch: Part Two.

Judges are smart and they might just ask you very directly what you want, or what's important to you right now. Be fully prepared with your elevator pitch on what you do. Follow that with a list of at least three things you could use advice on, e.g. advancing your skills, acquiring new clients, and any "tricks of the trade" they have noticed over the years that may not have occurred to you. These three are generic open-ended requests.

If you need the judge's advice on something specific that's currently pending, be sensitive about that. If the judge keeps steering the conversation back to you, fine, but if not, wait at least a few days after the lunch, and only after the judge has received a handwritten personal note of thanks from you, then call. Thank the judge again, and say you could really use some of their experience and insight on a matter, if the judge has a moment.

Good news! There's more than one retired judge.

Notes / Comments / Action Items:

Nobody can go back and start a new beginning, but anyone can start today and make a new ending.

-Maria Robinson

2. Ask your existing client(s) for a non-billable meeting to learn more about their business.

You'll blow their minds and garner mountains of respect, (which leads to more business).

Past and current clients are your best source for new business and new clients, but that's not the subject of this non-billable meeting. This is a rapport building session, preferably over lunch which you buy. Or have the meet at their place where they walk you through "the plant" to give you a better idea of what they do. Don't be surprised if the client says, "Hey, it just occurred to me, you might call Mike over at _____. He was just telling me he needed some legal advice." Or they might say, "... you know our CFO was telling me last week she was worried about some international import tax laws. Maybe your firm can review the situation and help set her mind at ease." This may come up over dessert or the second cup of coffee, so, don't book a meeting for two to three hours from the start of your meeting with the client. You don't want to have to rush off just when things were getting real chummy. You're not "cramming them in." No calls. No emails. No rushing off. It's all about them. They need to see, hear and feel that at their core.

The best Rainmakers have this mindset: they are always trying to help grow their client's business. Whenever possible actually send new business to your client. Think of your client. Now ask yourself, "How can I make their day?"

Worried about competition stealing your best clients? Tigers couldn't tear the client from their loyalty to your firm if you've referred some business to them!

Notes / Comments / Action Items:

Life is either a daring adventure or nothing.

- Helen Keller

3.   Show me the money.

Where is the money? Where is the money in your business?
Go there! Go there now. You know exactly what I mean.
Write down what / who immediately comes to mind now.

Notes / Comments / Action Items:

4.   Understand your product. What is it?
Understand your market. What is it?

What is the firm good at? What does the firm like to do?
Find out who wants or needs that for which you have a
passion.

Notes / Comments / Action Items:

5.1   Focus: Define the ideal client for each key practice area.

Then create a list of 30 defined prospects within each
practice area   and the best ways to communicate with
them?

Notes / Comments / Action Items:

**Life is like a
game of cards.
The hand that is dealt you
represents determinism; the
way you play it is free will.**

- Jawaharal Nehru

5.2. Focus: Construct profiles of your ideal clients.

Make a list of everyone who can hire your firm.

Everyone? At least a list of 500 companies, business types, people, etc. that fit your clients' profiles.

Research the people and companies that fit your "ideal client profile." Then, contact them by phone, and/or letter, and/or brochure, and/or advertising in the journals/media that they interact with, and/or one or more of the other methods outlined in this book.

Notes / Comments / Action Items:

5.3 Focus: Identify the firm's top five sources of revenue in terms of clients, client types, and practice areas.

Identify where 80% of the firms revenue has come from in the past five years.

What did you learn from analyzing this data?

Notes / Comments / Action Items:

5.4 Focus: Examine what's working. Do it, again.

Who else has the same needs as my current and past clients? Think. "Who pays me? Who pays me now, and who has paid me in the past? What need caused them to pay me? Who else has that need?"

Notes / Comments / Action Items:

After the game, the king and the pawn go into the same box.

- Italian proverb

6.1   Plan: Create a business development plan.

What's the plan?

Plan your work. Work your plan.

Go to pages 339 and 340 and fill out this business development plan form.

Notes / Comments / Action Items:

6.2   Plan: Create a business development checklist.

If you would like to get more info on how to create a biz dev check list go to page 341 and let the answers to the questions in the Expanded Business Development Quiz act as a guide to assist you in creating your personal customized business development plan.

Notes / Comments / Action Items:

6.3   Plan: Do now what has worked in the past.

How, specifically, did the firm acquire its past and current clients? Every client file should include a memo as to how the client came to choose your law practice. What steps did the firm take? How did that non-client become your client? What occurred? Take those same actions again.

Notes / Comments / Action Items:

Blessed are the flexible, for we shall not be bent out of shape.

- Anon

6.4 Plan: You must have biz dev time slots.

Crank up your biz dev machine with discipline.

Set aside four specific one-hour periods a week where you are speaking with a new business prospect.

And, if you aren't speaking with a prospect during any one of those four biz-dev-set-aside-time-slots, then you utilize that time slot to be actively engaged in one of the ideas in this book to secure a meeting with a prospect.

Identify four one-hour biz dev time slots a week right now.

Notes / Comments / Action Items:

6.5 Plan: Two titles for everyone.

Make sure everyone in your firm knows that he or she has "marketing co-director" as part of their title and job description.

Notes / Comments / Action Items:

6.6 Plan: Look at your new business and income budget plan daily, or at least weekly.

For a simple but good foundational guide to setting up a business plan you can google "wells fargo writing a business plan" or go to https://wellsfargobusinessinsights.com/business-stages/startup/writing-business-plan

Notes / Comments / Action Items:

You cannot dream yourself into a character; you must hammer and forge yourself one.

- Henry David Thoreau

6.7 Plan: Leverage business development tools and forms.

Use the Business Plan Action Sheets available at the back of the book as an organizing tool for annual, quarterly, monthly and weekly goals.

Use the Weekly Business Development Plan vs Actual form available at the back of the book as an organizing tool for quarterly or annual goals. See Table of Contents for the page numbers.

Periodically check the book's website for update articles and forms addressing your Business Development Plan.

Notes / Comments / Action Items:

6.8 Plan: Make a list of three actions you'll take this week to grow your business.

Then do the list.

Notes / Comments / Action Items:

6.9 Plan: Have a monthly business development meeting.

Have a monthly business development meeting assisted by the CMO, Chief Marketing Officer, and/or a business development consultant. Every two weeks is better.

Notes / Comments / Action Items

Sow an act, and you reap
a habit; sow a habit, and
you reap a character;
sow a character, and
you reap a destiny.

- George Dana Boardman

7.1 Hire a business development coach.

Does every firm member have a business development coach that they speak with confidentially, regularly, and who holds them accountable to their biz dev goals?

Hire a biz dev coach for firm partners and associates on an as needed basis. Good lawyers don't want to admit to anyone but a trusted coach in a confidential session that they are having "difficulty with anything that seems like selling," or that they are having difficulty with the elevator pitch.

The outside coach is in the best position to work confidentially with any firm lawyer afraid to seek inside help in these key business areas for fear of appearing "less than" to firm partners and others.

The best coaches understand those issues that can get in the way of an attorney conducting business development activities. Avoid all but the best coaches.

A skilled biz dev coach / consultant / trainer has decades of sales and marketing experience, is knowledgeable about the challenges of different legal markets, certified as an executive life coach, trained in personality types, understands time management, and, ideally, holds a masters in the science of neurolinguistics with the ability to recognize an old underlying belief system that is impeding greater business development success.

The best biz dev coaches know how to work seamlessly in concert with the Managing Partner and Chief Marketing Officer.

Notes / Comments / Action Items:

The only way of finding the limits of the possible is by going beyond them into the impossible.

- Arthur C. Clarke

7.2   Hire a business development coach: Part Two.

Law firms in the United States have not ignored this coaching phenomenon and are beginning to use coaches more strategically.

In a 2006 story in The Recorder, Northern California's leading legal newspaper, one commentator says coaching is also making an appearance on international law management radar screens. For example, in June 2006, the Ark Group, a leading British legal consulting firm and publisher of Managing Partner magazine, produced a full two-day seminar in London, UK on Coaching for Law Firms: Making it work! The Ark Group puts forward the following rationale for the conference:

"With clear evidence that executive and performance coaching is producing tangible organizational and individual benefits in a wide range of sectors, there is clearly accelerating interest within many legal practices to explore and invest in coaching and mentoring."

For a good national business development consulting and coaching firm go to the book's web site, www.kbdag.com, or contact the author.

See Executive Coaching ROI at end of book.

Notes / Comments / Action Items:

Address the "part" of the person you want to respond to you, not the part that is irritating you.

- Neuroscience Research

7.3 Hire a business development coach: consultant-trainer. Part three.

For the latest contact information of a national firm that can consult you on business development techniques as well as provide you (and your associates) with individualized executive level coaching in overcoming any challenge that may be holding you (them) back, go to the book's web site, www.kbdag.com, or contact the author.

Some challenges are conscious. Other challenges may be just below your level of awareness but can be easily brought to your attention and effectively addressed in a short amount of time with the right executive coach.

The best certified executive coaches understand those "issues" that can get in the way of an attorney conducting business development activities.

Make sure every attorney has the phone number of a business development consultant / coach who can support them with fully confidential conversations in creating and achieving their biz dev goals.

Make sure every attorney not meeting his business development goals has a meeting with his business development coach within thirty days.

See Executive Coaching ROI at end of book.

Notes / Comments / Action Items:

Most adults are acting out the isomorphic structure of belief systems formed before the age of eight.

-Ancient Tree

7.4 Hire a business development coach: the ROI of executive coaching.

A Fortune 500 study by MetrixGlobal reported "a 529% return on (coaching) investment and significant intangible benefits to the business."

A recent article about executive coaching stated "... 92% of leaders being coached say they plan to use a coach again."

Most lawyers don't want to admit to anyone but a trusted outside coach in a confidential session that they are having "difficulty selling", or, that they need "help with the elevator pitch".

Establish an annual business development strategy. Break it into 52 weekly increments for the firm and monthly outcomes for each associate and partner. A well trained business development coach who is an executive life coach trained at the masters level in neurolinguistics can help members in a confidential session overcome those individual challenges that get in the way of achieving their revenue enhancement timelines. Review the Art and Science of Selling section in the book, and verify everyone has some version of the Business Development Action Sheet printed in the book.

Notes / Comments / Action Items:

We are what we repeatedly do. Excellence, therefore, is not an act but a habit.

- Aristotle

7.5 Hire a business development coach: Leverage the ROI of Executive Coaching.

Investigate the return on investment of executive coaching.

Executive consulting /coaching is already a big trend in corporate America.

According to Fortune magazine, executive coaching has developed as one of the hottest management tools in recent years. "It is a grassroots movement that is spreading in some of the unlikeliest corners of Corporate America, including IBM, AT&T, and Kodak."

No small wonder. A recent study about executive coaching for a Fortune 500 firm by MetrixGlobal, reported "a 529% return on investment and significant intangible benefits to the business."

Support for a similar high level of ROI is found in other consulting/coaching studies. And the use of executive coaching does not appear to be "a flash in the pan." A recent 2006 study about coaching in Fast Company [Online] states, "63% of organizations say they plan to increase their use of coaching over the next five years. Most telling, 92% of leaders being coached say they plan to use a coach again. Both indicate strong endorsements of coaching: the first by the organizations paying the bills, and the second by the leaders who are actually receiving coaching."

Notes / Comments / Action Items:

You cannot plough a field by turning it over in your mind.

-Anon

7.6 Hire a business development coach: Leverage the ROI of Executive Coaching: Part Two.

Fast Company [Online] states, "But as coaches become a more commonplace fixture in American law firms, their roles are becoming more structured. Some firms have begun formal coaching programs for associates and junior partners to navigate the thorny transition from service lawyer to business getter. Others have brought in coaches to help their most senior leadership deal with issues as vital as client retention and as solemn as succession planning.

The growth of coaching within law firms is fuelled by the recognition that many lawyers in developing their management and marketing skills, respond more positively to one-to-one/small group-based coaching than to team/large group-based learning."

All lawyers in the firm, regardless of current level of performance, should see coaching as a means to take them to a higher level of success than they can achieve on their own. Coaching will make what is good in their practice -- even better. Sound coaching is designed to grow people's strengths and to develop their individual talents. To draw an analogy, most professional athletes would never dream of competing without the assistance of a coach who will stretch them to attain peak performance. Why wouldn't lawyers want the same advantage?

And in today's competitive environment, coaching is growing to become a critical part of building and maintaining a thriving legal practice. From Google online: "Jim Cranston, director of business development at Pillsbury Winthrop Shaw Pitman, a firm of 900 lawyers, comments: 'This has gotten quite popular...my own take is that is looking for an edge, an advantage.' "

Notes / Comments / Action Items:

We must take time to understand what motivates us, and, in many cases, the answer comes in response to the two questions, "What are we moving away from, or seeking to avoid? And what are we moving toward, or seeking to have more of, or new in our life?"

- *Neuroscience Research*

7.7 Hire a business development coach: Know the difference between biz dev coaches and marketing agents.

Marketing agents focus on brand name promotion. Marketing agents use advertising and external projects to promote the firm to third parties and may never communicate with actual firm members. An Executive Business Development Coach works at the individual level in one-on-one or group settings.

A Business Development Coach can help with sales training and help individual attorneys track progress against biz dev targets. The really good Biz Dev coaches thoroughly understand marketing and advertising because they have been in those fields with hands on media experience including writing and directing TV and radio spots.

A Business Development Coach combines sales training with biz dev consulting. The better ones should have the additional skills of a certified Executive Coach trained in high level co-active personal coaching.

An Executive Business Development Coach combines the skills of a Business Development Consultant along with those of a Certified Executive Coach experienced in working with Senior Partners and Managing General Partners whose responsibilities go well beyond those of an individual associate attorney.

The author prefers coaches who can leverage neuroscience research and have attained a master's certification in neurolinguistic programming. It's a bonus if the Business Development Coach is also a Certified Mediator, a skill that can help calm the waters when an attorney is feeling angry or overwhelmed by his biz dev budget.

For the latest research and articles on the ROI of Executive Coaching for yourself and lawyers in the firm go to www.100WaysToGrowAThrivingLawPractice.com.

Notes / Comments / Action Items:

Inaction breeds doubt and fear. Action breeds confidence and courage. If you want to conquer fear, do not sit home and think about it. Go out and get busy.

- Dale Carnegie

8.1 Sound bite: Give your "elevator pitch" to everyone.

Tell every friend, club member and business contact something like, "Our law firm has some excess capacity. We're accepting new clients now, and would welcome referrals."

Be sure to give them a promotional sound bite like, "and you probably know we specialize in...." (Fill in the blank with your well honed elevator pitch in 15 to 30 seconds).

Then add, "And I'm not sure I mentioned some of our more stellar accomplishments like .... (mention two in 30 seconds)...." Do all of this in 60 to 90 seconds max. Unless they beg for more.

How is your 15 second "elevator pitch"? One sentence or two that summarizes the firm's specialty. And one sentence that includes a hook.

A "hook" is a teaser that heightens curiosity and increases the likelihood of a follow-up call. Something like, "Call me any time for a free exploratory discussion and be sure to ask me how we saved a business like yours four million dollars." Or, "Next time we speak, if we have time, ask me about my date with writer Danielle Steel." [A line this author can use.]

Notes / Comments / Action Items:

**It is always in the last lap that races are gained or lost.
The effort must be forthcoming.
This is no moment to slacken.**

-    *Winston Churchill*

8.2   Sound bite: Give your "elevator pitch" to everyone: Part Two.

Contact every business acquaintance? Yes. Banker, stock broker, CPA, insurance agents, priest, rabbi, minister, meditation instructor, yoga teacher, doctor, mailperson, electrician, club President, building manager, restaurant owner/manager, City Councilman, Mayor, Congressman, U.S. Senator, every luncheon speaker and trade show presenter, hairdresser, manicurist, barber, law professors and your law professors' contacts. Everyone.

You give most of these people a lot of business. Let them know that the firm has "excess capacity" and want to fill that capacity and stay on the hiring side, rather than laying off anyone. This will allow your firm to better support building the community's economy, and to better support the church (synagogue, temple, or yoga center). These contacts know a lot of people, and they know the pain of "excess capacity."

Look for any excuse to send these folks, or anyone else, a birthday card, or congratulations card. Your first objective is to be perceived as kind, considerate, and sensitive to detail. Your overriding goal is to be the "top of mind" attorney who pops into their brain when that person thinks about lawyers, or is included whenever that person is asked for a legal referral. When you send a note, or card, make it personal.
No business card or press release. Wait 60 days then send the press release, with a note saying, "Hope your birthday (or restaurant opening, or _____) was the best. Here's what I've (my firm has) been up to. Always room for more business and your great business development ideas."

Notes / Comments / Action Items:

Do not wait to strike till the iron is hot; but make it hot by striking.

- William B. Sprague

8.3   Sound bite: Become a video movie star.

Video yourself.

In the privacy of your own home or office, tape record yourself giving your 15 second one line elevator pitch, and your 30 second, 1 minute, and 3 minute summary business descriptions.

It's easy. You can purchase a very low-cost video cam that clips on the top of your computer screen and has a simple USB plug for power and connectivity.

Logitech has a simple super low-cost clip on / pivotal video cam with a simple USB plug. Or put your cell phone's video cam on a box or shelf to make the video.

When you play it back, ask yourself, "Would I hire that attorney?"

Take consolation in the fact that the most famous academy award winners had to practice, practice, and practice.

A very pro-active CMO might hand you the Logitech video cam and ask you to email her your various elevator pitches by the end of next week. So, be prepared.

Notes / Comments / Action Items:

8.4   Sound bite: Hone your elevator pitch.

Are the words "frcc" and "no charge" always included in the first sentence or two when discussing that first consult with a prospective client?

Notes / Comments / Action Items:

Even if you're on the right track, you'll get run over if you just sit there.

- Will Rogers

8.5   Sound bite: Be loud and clear that your first exploratory conversation is "FREE" and "NO CHARGE."

It's worth repeating. Make sure the words "free" and "no charge" and "no obligation" are always included in the first sentence when discussing an initial consult with a prospective client.

Use the words "free" and "no charge" in the last sentence with any new prospect. Lawyers are not famous for being low cost. So, make that first approach by a prospective client as easy as possible.

You can always say the initial exploratory meeting or phone call to help them define what legal services they may or may not need is FREE and there will be no bill if they don't use the firm's services.

When referring you to others you can bet they will tell their friends that there is no charge for the first exploratory meeting. You need that free word-of-mouth advertising to grow your business.

Optionally, after "x" number of free minutes and the legal needs have been fairly well defined, you can discreetly say would they like you to now become a formal and hired advocate for their needs?

Notes / Comments / Action Items:

It astonishes me how much being kind enhances our beauty.

- Kathleen L Murry

9.1 Leverage NSR: Ask each client and prospect, "What's important to you?"

NSR, neuroscience research, is the growing science of how those synaptic connections influence us and other organisms.

"What's important to you?" That question utilizes well researched NSR and actually taps into your client's or prospect's conscious and unconscious decision-making process.

Forty years of neurolingistic research and the wisdom of Carol Bartz, CEO, goes into this question.

Does every file have the client's or prospect's answer to, "What's important to you?" The client's and prospect's every decision will be made from that platform, either consciously or unconsciously. You MUST know what that platform is and direct EVERY communication to that pleasure-pain, fight-flight, love-hate, move toward- move away from, command and control center.

For more on key motivators you must be aware of, go to www.100WaysToGrowAThrivingLawPractice.com/ articles.

Notes / Comments / Action Items:

9.2 Leverage NSR: Ask yourself, "What's important to me?"

Ask every member of your firm, including (and especially) the front desk receptionist, "What's important to you?"

Notes / Comments / Action Items:

Let me tell you the secret that has led me to my goal. My strength lies solely in my tenacity.

- Louis Pasteur

9.3 Leverage NSR: Know the science of rapport building.

Are all of our attorneys familiar with NLP, neurolinguistic programming, and NLP's research on rapport building and motivation creation? If not, locate a more in-depth discussion. Search NLP in the book Index, or send an email to this author requesting the information.

Notes / Comments / Action Items:

9.4 Leverage NSR: Learn NLP rapport techniques.

If you haven't learned the neurolinguistic programming (NLP) rapport technique, your competitor has. These have been proven to work over and over again.

Do firm members know how to increase the probability that a prospect, client, judge, or jury will fall-in-like with them in just a few minutes? Learn art and science of rapport.

For more info, go to www.100WaysToGrowAThrivingLawPractice.com/ articles.

Notes / Comments / Action Items:

Twenty years from now you will be
more disappointed by the things
that you didn't do than by
the ones you did do.
So throw off the bowlines.
Sail away from the safe harbor.
Catch the trade winds in your sails.
Explore. Dream. Discover.

- Mark Twain

9.5 Leverage NSR: Use well researched focusing language.

For a reminder of the 5 key elemental questions in defining a Goal and the 12 "mental system checks" to ferret out any "hidden" issues go to www.100WaysToGrowAThrivingLawPractice.com/articles.

You must know the latest research and key rules behind a well-formed Goal, or Desired Outcome, when supporting a client or prospect to come up with a well-defined Objective.

When running a goal-setting meeting, be sure to know the communication techniques based on the last three decades of advanced neurolinguistic programming (NLP) and supporting research.

Have an NLP master explain how to ask a client key questions to ascertain their decision-making strategy, and how to fully define a desired legal outcome.

To reach a master level NLP professional, go to www.100WaysToGrowAThrivingLawPractice.com.

Notes / Comments / Action Items:

9.6 Leverage NSR: Proper acknowledgement wins friends and new business.

Have an NLP master explain how to fully acknowledge a job well done so that it lands with maximum beneficial impact. Each person has their own unique way to "know" they're appreciated. Some need to see a little note, some need to hear words of thanks, and others need a pat on the shoulder or back (a touch). Others prefer the smell of flowers, or the taste of something sweet. In most cases, it's best to combine as many of the five key sensory receptors as possible.

Notes / Comments / Action Items:

Press on!
A better fate
awaits thee.

- Victor Hugo

9.7   Leverage NSR: Use key motivational words in promotional material, websites and bylines.

The most popular word in the English language is "FREE." So, be sure to use FREE and "all communication is privileged and attorney-client confidential."

Other key words or phrases: cost effective, personal attention, efficient, flexible, specialized representation, resources, unique, special client services, and prompt individual attention. All of these help to generate the highest quality of reputation.

Amongst other statements in one firm's radio spot is this line: "You have rights, and we represent those rights." That line feels good to many because it has neurolinguistic associative connectivity built into the phraseology.

As a rule, make sure every ad has the 3 primary predicate types included: visual, auditory, and kinesthetic. See Neurolinguistic Programming, NLP, research that discusses this elsewhere in Book. Or go to www.100WaysToGrowAThrivingLawPractice.com/ articles. Look up the art and science of rapport.

Notes / Comments / Action Items:

9.8   Leverage NSR: Learn from the masters.

Look at every AmLaw 100 website for any unique images, powerful words and phrases, special marketing features, attractive structure and useful links. Some have discovered the added value of motion. Notice, though, how few have latched on to the YouTube phenom and have a home page video mini-movie screen with a click-start button.

Notes / Comments / Action Items:

In absence of clearly defined goals, we become strangely loyal to performing daily acts of trivia.

- Author unknown

9.9 Leverage NSR: Make sure every job well done by a firm member is acknowledged properly.

For the "Art of Praise" go to www.100WaysToGrowAThriving LawPractice.com/ ArtOfPraise

Once you pat someone on the back for a job well done, and after you make sure they really get it, wait a few beats then add, "Again congratulations, and so, what's next on your successful agenda?"

Praise lawyers for a job well done at every opportunity. Remember what Carol Bartz, CEO of Yahoo, said, "I have the puppy theory ... quick feedback." So, the positive psychological reinforcement is closely associated with the behavior.

As much as you can, let each lawyer know they are a proven success story who will continually cause your firm to grow and prosper. People will want to grow the business of a place that treats them like a treasure.

Notes / Comments / Action Items:

While they were saying among themselves it cannot be done, it was done.

- Helen Keller

9.10 Leverage NSR: Become an expert at the NLP Reframe.

If you don't know what an NLP "Reframe" is, ask yourself how many clients, judges, or juries would you have liked to have "reframed," then get real curious and go to www.100WaysToGrowAThrivingLawPractice.com/articles.

By reviewing the NLP material, you can receive for free, that extra little skill that can help you win that extra client, or that next negotiation. In all cases, understanding NLP can improve the important relationships in your life, e.g. business relationships, parents, spouse, your intended and your child.

There are obvious reframes, and then there are those subtle, yet powerfully effective reframes.

Notes / Comments / Action Items:

9.11 Leverage NSR: Leverage holidays and holy days.

Think of ways to highlight (leverage) national holidays and generate activities (advantage) during other holidays like New Years.

Be sensitive during certain holy days, e.g. Christmas, Easter, Hanukah, Yom Kippur, Muharram, Ramadan, etc.

Add religious affiliation on your contact's information in your data base, and make sure all company calendars reflect sensitive holy days.

Notes / Comments / Action Items:

Rather than thinking 'if and when', start doing, take action, stop talking about 'if and when'.

- Catherine Pulsifer

9.12 Leverage NSR: Use the new "feedback model" to maintain rapport with clients and prospects.

When providing constructive feedback make sure it is done within a tested and researched framework.

A new classic feedback model based on years of research has two elements:

"What I liked was ..." Or, "What I thought worked well was ..."

"And what I would like to see more of is ..."

You have to be clever here. "What I would like to see more of" is a soft way to say that you'd like to see alternative or additional behavior of a particular type without blatantly criticizing the person and thus ruin the opportunity for improvement by making the person defensive.

There are plenty of times where you can be blatantly critical. You'll know the difference based on the circumstances.

This same technique should be used with colleagues and employees and virtually all relationships where rapport and down stream cooperation is important.

Notes / Comments / Action Items:

Nothing in the world can take the place of persistence. Talent will not; nothing is more common than unsuccessful men with talent. Genius will not; unrewarded genius is almost a proverb. Education will not; the world is full of educated derelicts. Persistence and determination are omnipotent.

- Calvin Coolidge

10. The Rainmaker Formula.

Rainmakers and the top business development people around the Country all have two characteristics in common.

These two qualities are essential for any successful lawyer who wants to consistently "fill the pipe" with ongoing prospects and new business.

The two traits that every major business developer will exhibit: motivation and technique.

There are clearly defined and teachable methods to achieve these two elements. You cannot succeed without both.

For more information on the Rainmaker Formula and how to transfer that knowledge to yourself and other members of the firm, go to the book chapter tilted "The Art and Science of Selling."

For more information on this subject, go to www.100WaysToGrowAThrivingLawPractice.com/ articles.

Motivation and technique: one without the other will not succeed. For in-depth training for your law firm to build and harness these two essential characteristics, go to www.100WaysToGrowAThrivingLawPractice.com/ articles.

Notes / Comments / Action Items:

Knowing is not enough,
we must apply.
Willing is not enough,
we must do.

- Johann von Goethe

11. Interview Rainmakers.

Interview the Rainmakers in your firm. Ask them how they do it? Which techniques can be taught to others?

If you are not a Rainmaker and don't have one in your firm, find one to interview. How? Contact the author, or join LMA, Legal Marketing Association, and ask the LMA President to introduce you to one.

For the closest LMA Chapter President near you, go to www.100WaysToGrowAThrivingLawPractice.com/ links.

There is a strategy developed within neuroscience research on how to "elicit" a "strategy of competency". It can be taught but is too lengthy for this book. In summary it involves finding out what the competent person is doing, thinking, feeling and most importantly what that person's foundational guiding beliefs in addition to motivation and technique.

For more information on this technique, contact the author or, go to www.100WaysToGrowAThrivingLawPractice.com/ articles.

Notes / Comments / Action Items:

Don't wait for your "ship to come in," and feel angry and cheated when it doesn't. Get going with something small.

- Irene Kassorla

12. The lawyer down the hall is working with your next client.

You just don't know it, yet.

Network intra-firm.

Make sure the IP specialist working with Company "X" supports you in connecting with other departments within that Company "X".

For example, ask your IP expert if an introduction or query can be made to all the other departments at Company X as to whether they have any other legal needs that might be served by the firm's other practice areas, e.g. tax, litigation, contracts, mediation, labor, employee, import, industry legislation watch, etc.

Naturally, the IP attorney is taking a risk at letting someone come in who might "turn off" the client.

But a worse scenario is for the IP specialist to lose the client because a competitor came in through Company X's tax department and then used that rapport to leverage in their own IP specialist.

The more inroads into an account the more likely the account will remain loyal to the firm.

As much as Frank in IP wants to horde his special cash cow, he runs a greater risk of someone poaching his cow and putting their brand on it unless the account has multiple reasons to fend off competitive advances and is having all of its legal needs met by Frank's colleagues.

Notes / Comments / Action Items:

An ounce of action is worth a ton of theory.

- Friedrich Engels

13.   **What's your competitor doing?**

If you respect what they're doing to grow business, you can do it, too.

Notes / Comments / Action Items:

14.   **Let your competitor's clients' competition list become your prospect list.**

In column "A", list your competitor's clients. In column "B" make a list of companies competing with those clients.

How many in column "B" are potential clients of yours?

Once you have made a client of one your competitor's client's competitors, this will give you more leverage in winning over those clients in the "A" column, as well.

Continue asking the question, "Why aren't my competitor's clients my clients?"

Notes / Comments / Action Items:

15.   **Identify leading lawyers in the community.**

How did they become the "leading lawyers?" How are they maintaining their leading lawyer status? Imitate their best qualities. Be a success investigator, a success detective.

Notes / Comments / Action Items:

They will rise highest who strive for the highest place.
(Altius ibunt qui as summa nituntur.)

- Latin Proverb

16.1   Just ask: use the "soft ask" with friends.

The "soft ask" is very low-key business development.

Tell every friend, club member and business contact that your firm "... is accepting new clients, and would welcome any referrals."

Most people don't go around thinking about how to bring the firm new business, but now some will, at least for 30 seconds, possibly a lot more.

Thirty seconds of mind space is very valuable. That's why a short TV or radio spot costs so much.

Make a list of friends, club members, association members, church acquaintances, car pool buddies, and relatives who'd have no problem with you slipping in the news that your business is accepting new clients, especially if you've cleverly sandwiched in that subject amongst other topics.

But don't gloss over the subject. Allow it to marinate a little by adding at least one client success story.

Tell a joke first [see the book Index for a link to fresh daily jokes] and follow that with, "Oh, by the way, our law firm is accepting new clients, and would welcome any referrals. Our tax department just saved this one company $500,000, and our intellectual property department just won a case for a small client up against one of the Internet giants. Oh gosh, now I'll probably have to buy you lunch for all your referrals." Pause. Give them time to say something. But be ready with a topic of mutual interest to help wrap up the conversation.

Notes / Comments / Action Items:

Action is the foundational key to all success.

- Anthony Robbins

16.2 Just ask: incorporate the "blatant ask" frequently.

Use the "blatant ask" to an easy and grateful audience, your vendors. This is a flat out, unambiguous, request for new business referrals. Withstanding all the ABA Model Rules of Professional Conduct and those of the State Bars within which you are registered, you can approach every one of your vendors and let them know that you have room for additional clients and ask them if they know of anyone your firm might be able to assist. Explain that you're prohibited from paying them a referral fee or any quid pro quo. Provide them with an elevator pitch about your firm and the value you have provided to others. Remind them that the first consultation is always free with no obligation. For example, you could say, "Can you think of any new clients for us *now* that would help us maintain, or expand, our current level of services?" Your vendors will scratch their heads and try and come up with a few referrals right there on the spot. At a minimum you will periodically rise to "top of mind" as they go about their business, and speak with their friends. It helps if you've used the powerfully suggestive word "now" when making your request. For an expanded discussion of how to leverage mildly suggestive language techniques and neuroscience research in this area go to this book's website. Vendors know plenty of other business people. All of whom need legal services at some point for something. Remember, you're doing the vendors a favor by asking because they need your business to be stable and hopefully to grow, and by extension, without any promises or quid pro quo, their business just might, as a result, grow, as well.

Notes / Comments / Action Items:

Ideas without action are worthless.

- Helen Keller

17.1 **Conduct fifteen Gold Mine Interviews.**

If this is the only action you take from this book, you will have received more than a 1,000% Return On Investment.

This is your gold mine activity. Interview fifteen professional idea generators for hire.

Interview these fifteen companies, each one specializing in making you rich and famous.

Generate an explosion of free ideas by interviewing three different companies in five different categories: three advertising firms, three marketing firms, three public relations firms, three event planners, and three business brochure writers. Ask each how they would grow your net revenue. And then, listen. Keep asking, "How, specifically?"

Immediately after the interview sit down and type up every idea that came out of that meeting. Note what you can do in the next meeting to make it even more productive for you.

Yes, this will take time. And yes, it cannot help but increase your business because of all the ideas that will be floated by you. These people are full time idea experts. Three to five ideas each meeting times fifteen meetings means forty-five to seventy-five biz dev ideas for you.

Each interviewed company will pummel you with requests about your skills and goals forcing you to get your act totally together, an immediate short term win.

See Ways #18.1 and 18.2 on preparing for these Goldmine Interviews.

Notes / Comments / Action Items:

**Sometimes the
highest price in the world
is doing nothing.
A lot of people do nothing wrong.
They do nothing.
And that's what's wrong.**

- Ben Feldman

17.2 Conduct fifteen Gold Mine Interviews: Part Two.

First, ask the business promotion company to tell you what they've done for other law firms. Second, ask what business promotion ideas they've used that worked for another category of business that could also work for yours. Take notes.

Some interviewees will delay giving you their ideas for your specific firm saying they need to know more about your market and competition. Some will ask for a research budget to study your market and competition. Simply say you can probably answer most of their research questions right now, "What are they?" Ask, "What specifically do they need to know," before telling you what they can do for you? Tell them you are in "x" legal service market(s), and there are "y" law firms competing for the same business. Define what you believe are the ideal clients for these "x" markets. Then you ask, "Now, how is your company going to connect me with paying clients?"

All of these companies know the risk is that you'll take their ideas and go with someone else. It's a loss leader, a normal business casualty. Your firm does the same thing. A prospect comes in and wants to know what you can do for them and you tell them. Some become paying clients, others don't. It's the same with these fifteen professional grow-your-business companies.

Brochure writers specializing in writing and creating promotional material for law firms will be familiar with your needs. And they will have a good idea on what has and hasn't work in the past. The brochure vignettes for each practice area become the basis for the summaries on the firm's website which must use key words to enhance your SEO, search engine optimization.

Notes / Comments / Action Items:

Fortify yourself with contentment, for this is an impregnable fortress.

- Epictetus

17.3 Conduct fifteen Gold Mine Interviews: Part Three. Turn each Gold Mine Interviewee into a potential investor.

Don't bulls... these professional business promotion experts during your conversations. Be honest. Tell them, "Until my business grows, my budget is very limited, to say the least. But, I may create a line item in the budget for your company going forward, if I can justify it." (In the back of your mind you may fund a project from existing funds, bringing in an investor, or taking out a business loan if their proposal demonstrates sufficient ROI, return on investment.)

And tell them, "If your actions are successful in a phase one project, then I will be able to increase my budget for your services in a phase two project." Be straightforward and say you are meeting with a number of companies offering to grow your business. That should wet their competitive appetite.

It's rare, but not impossible, that one of the fifteen promotional firms is so convinced of their ability to grow your business, that they will take the job on a contingency basis. This will assume access to your books through a known and trusted confidential CPA source. (To keep your total books confidential, but allow for a fair assessment of business growth upon which to pay a contingency fee, you can have their CPA and your CPA select a neutral 3rd party CPA who is only authorized to report net growth revenue, and from what sources, if that is applicable.) Don't hesitate to casually mention this option to every proposer as "it came up in another interview."

Notes / Comments / Action Items:

Perseverance is king.

- Josh Billings

17.4 Conduct fifteen Gold Mine Interviews: Part Four.

Take immediate action on your Gold Mine Interviews.

Begin implementing the ideas generated during the fifteen interviews with these business promotion experts.

If you can afford one or more of the promotional budgets presented, great, because now you'll be able to supplement the strategy of the hired firm with all the other ideas you personally came up with during the overall interview process, along with those presented to you that you want to utilize.

If you cannot afford to hire any of the firms "until our business grows," tell them that.

Ideally, you do something that proves you are for real. Go with someone, even if it's a low cost ghost writer to help you write just one article. This way you can gently turn down all the other business proposals "for the moment" so, that you later can "come back" to a selected marketing / advertising /PR firm "with something to hand out as a credibility piece as a first step before expanding into larger marketing activities."

You need to end up on each interviewee's good side. Use your very valuable legal consulting services to your advantage when delivering unpleasant news.

Give each interviewee a chit for a free legal consulting session for them, or one of their friends, or family members. If done right, you've calmed the waters, secured many brilliant business development ideas for free, polished your business image and pitch with every meeting, and created fifteen potential prospects by offering each interviewee a free legal discussion which you would do normally, anyway. Win. Win. Win.

Notes / Comments / Action Items:

Don't fix the blame, fix the mistake.

-Anon

18.1 Prepare for the big Gold Mine Interviews: Step One.

Prepare for the big Gold Mine Interviews with smaller Gold Mine Interviews.

Here's a secret way to get prepared for your bigger ticket Gold Mine Interviews indentified in Way #17.

Interview the head of advertising sales for a cable TV station and ask that person how their cable TV station could grow your net revenue. Do this same interview with a local newspaper ad manager, a local radio station commercial sales director, one Regional (or State wide) magazine publication display ad sales person, and one national publication display ad sales director. Ask each one how advertising in their medium will grow your business.

After six of these phone calls, you'll be a much smarter interviewer for the larger advertising and marketing companies.

When you toss out a few media advertising "stats" the bigger players will know to step up their game, minimize the jive, and cut out some of the fluff in their budgets.

Go to the Yellow Pages, Bing, or Google and make a list right now of all the media outlets in the area(s) covered by the firm. If you're super busy, assign this research task to a university student majoring in advertising.

Notes / Comments / Action Items:

"Never believe that a few caring people can't change the world. For, indeed, they are the only ones who ever have."

- Margaret Mead

18.2 Prepare for the Gold Mine Interviews: Step Two.

Utilize this trick of the trade.

Another important tactic: when you call XYZ advertising or marketing company, first ask for the owner, or president. Do NOT settle for a sales rep in that first conversation.

If the owner or president is not in then leave that specific person a very short message saying you wish to discuss hiring their firm to grow your legal business. Tell the owner who you are and what you want.

Initially, let "the boss" deal with you directly or refer you down to the "rep" for your industry or geographic area. You always want to deal with the boss, or someone that was referred to you by their boss. In many cases the rep won't know how well you know his boss but the rep will certainly be on his or her best behavior in any case putting forth their best effort. And the rep will smile politely if you have to "temporarily" put their proposal on the side burner.

The Chief Marketing Officer is perfectly qualified to do these Gold Mine Interviews (GMI's) and will have done all or some portion of them already.

For more GMI preparation see Way #45: Utilize FREE research and ideas from direct mail companies.

Notes / Comments / Action Items:

I can live for two months on a compliment.

- Mark Twain

19.   Utilize FREE research and ideas from direct mail companies.

This Way could easily be Way #18 Step 3 in preparing for your fifteen Gold Mine Interviews covered in Way #17.

Many mail houses will provide you with FREE research on your target audience to attract your business. Interview at least 3 direct mail houses and notice how much smarter you become about your business. They will provide you with FREE market research, FREE samples of designs and styles that have worked in the past. They will provide you with FREE copy suggestions. It's as if you subcontracted an advertising team but their initial work and promotional ideas are FREE. Tell the direct mail rep, "We might try a very limited and very low-cost test toward a very small specific targeted audience."

Again, going through this short exercise with the direct mail companies will be a low stress way to prepare you for the interviews with the bigger marketing, advertising and public relations companies.

Notes / Comments / Action Items:

20.   Goal: Distribute seven business cards a week.

Track this on your calendar. Have some fun with this, and provide yourself with little rewards for achieving new levels of business card promotion.

You'll also start to note that there are more opportunities to hand out your card than you first thought.

Notes / Comments / Action Items:

"What lies behind us and what lies before us are small matters compared to what lies within us."

- Ralph Waldo Emerson

21. More FREE marketing ideas.

Direct mail. Tried but true.

Many direct mail houses will provide you with FREE research on your target audience to attract your business. Interview at least 3 direct mail house and notice how much smarter you become about your business. They will provide you with FREE market research, FREE samples of designs and styles that have worked in the past. They will provide you with FREE copy suggestions. It's as if you subcontracted an advertising team but their initial work and promotional ideas are FREE.

Go to a least 3 direct mail services for free research and free quotes.

Don't make it a sell piece. Make it a PUBLIC SERVICE memo, a problem / solution piece.

Notes / Comments / Action Items:

22. Inculcate the new biz dev mantra, "Everyone, everyone, everyone is a possible source of new business."

Nearly everyone is a potential source of new revenue for your firm, either directly or through their network of contacts.

Notes / Comments / Action Items:

To achieve maximum value with the brain, as with real estate, you must apply highest and best use.

- *Neuroscience Research*

23. Interview 10 local event planners.

These folks work with the wealthy and connected. Unless you are only trying to reach the impoverished, then talk to these folks. Use the "rapport" skills you can learn by going to the NLP section on the book's website, go to www.100WaysToGrowAThrivingLawPractice.com/ articles.

Ask each one how they would promote your business. If each provides 3 local event ideas, do the math, 3 x 10 = 30.

These event professionals have just given you 30 good ways to grow your business. Hire one. Be respectful when you get back to the others. Let them know it was a very, very difficult choice and because they are obviously extremely talented , you would like to keep them in mind for the next event.

Remember, each one of these business professionals is a potential client, and, amongst the group of them, know most of the movers and shakers in the community, i.e. your prospective clients. And be sure to offer each one a chit for one FREE exploratory legal discussion for themselves, a family member, or business associate.

If you see an opening to provide an incentive for any business referrals from them to you, you can approach it very circumspectly at first. These folks are smart. Referrals are their stock in trade and they live and die based on referrals. When you talk "referrals" you are talking their talk.

Invite them to be on your e-zine email list.

Notes / Comments / Action Items:

Twenty years from now you will be more disappointed by the things that you didn't do than by the ones you did do.

- Mark Twain

24.1   Join LMA: Join the Legal Marketing Association.

Then have lunch with the LMA chapter President. Ask the President for suggestions on growing your business.

Check out the resources of your local Legal Marketing Association (LMA).

If you don't have a Chief Marketing Officer, then check with the local or national Legal Marketing Association (LMA) list of free lance law firm marketing experts and business development consultants / coaches. See website below for contact info. Most freelance LMA members will provide you with a free business development proposal. Always ask, "What specifically will you do to grow my firm's business?" And, "What specifically will you do that is different from someone else?" More free ideas.

For LMA contact info, go to:
100WaysToGrowAThrivingLawPractice.com/
LegalMarketingAssoc

Notes / Comments / Action Items:

24.2   Join LMA: LMA is a must as a foundational resource.

To reach LMA, Legal Marketing Association, go to www.100WaysToGrowAThrivingLawPractice.com/ Links.

Besides belonging to the LMA, consider these other two marketing orgs:
Society of Competitive Intelligence Professionals based in Virginia, and Professional Services Marketing Group, based in the UK. For more info, go to www.100WaysToGrowAThrivingLawPractice.com/ Links

Notes / Comments / Action Items:

Inaction breeds doubt and fear. Action breeds confidence and courage. If you want to conquer fear, do not sit home and think about it. Go out and get busy.

- Dale Carnegie

25.   Have lunch with the President.

Ask for a lunch meeting with the President of the Chamber of Commerce.

The President of the Chamber of Commerce will almost always make time for a coffee, drink, or lunch, especially with a new member bringing in his or her annual dues.

The Chamber will be most focused on you between your first call and when you hand in your first check. Take advantage of that window where they are still selling you, and most interested in doing what it takes to bring you into the fold. They are measured on numbers. They need you to join. Make them work for it just a little. In fact, most relish the opportunity to help you grow your business.

Of course, you need to be a member of your local Chamber of Commerce. The Chamber's job description is to grow your business. Give them that opportunity. Tell every Chamber member what you do specifically and who are your ideal clients. Give the President a few business cards and a few three-fold glossy brochures. Don't be bashful. Brag. Give him testimonials and client success stories he can quote to his contacts. Use the words "free" and "no charge" for any initial discussion.

Over lunch ask the President if he, the Chamber, or a Chamber member could use some of your legal expertise.

Notes / Comments / Action Items:

Knowing is not enough, we must apply. Willing is not enough, we must do.

- Johann von Goethe

26. Have coffee with a legal editor.

Take a writer for a legal newspaper or legal column to lunch. Take writers for legal magazines to lunch. There's more than one.

Take a legal publication editor, and/or publisher and/or writer to lunch for all the obvious reasons. But make the talk about THEIR needs, what THEY see as key issues, what THEY believe are the tipping points and critical areas needing attention. Ask how your firm can help THEM. Can your firm help them with future articles, or a specific research in your area of expertise? How can you make their life easier, and /or increase their circulation, and/or address his / her needs, ambitions, goals, and personal passions in the legal world? Ask, "What's important to you?"

Hey, they're smart. They know what's what. But they don't know it all, and they know that, too. Make it about them. How did a nice person like them get into the carnivorous legal world? Just kidding. How can your firm and your contacts help them with their job? Let them know you know something about "x", and if they ever need research or a comment in the area of "x" to call you anytime. You'll do everything you can to help them meet a deadline.

Notes / Comments / Action Items:

**Nobody can go back and start
a new beginning, but anyone
can start today and make
a new ending.**

- Maria Robinson

27.1 Network: Tap into your natural network.

It is worth re-emphasizing.

Inculcate the idea that everyone, everyone, everyone is a possible source of business, or business referral. Send out the occasional memo reminding everyone in the firm that their next conversation with the mail person, bartender, waiter, or taxi driver could just bring in "the next big one."

Notes / Comments / Action Items:

27.2 Network: Hairdressers are your best friend.

Don't forget to ask your hairdresser / barber for any business referrals. Ask yourself how many people they are talking to every week. When someone is having their hair or nails done, both parties are looking for something of interest to discuss. Give them something of interest to discuss ... about you.

Give your hairdresser (barber) a stack of ten business card sized clear plastic holders that hold two cards: your business card and a FREE $5 Starbucks gift card (a "set"). Authorize the hairdresser to give one "set" to any client who needs a FREE exploratory consultation with an attorney. And she gives one to herself for everyone she gives out. And you give out a discount coupon provided by your hairdresser (barber) to people who would like one. These are independent voluntary actions and not quid pro quo.

Voluntary Reciprocal Referral Relationships. (TRIPLE R)

Notes / Comments / Action Items:

In absence of clearly defined goals, we become strangely loyal to performing daily acts of trivia.

- Author unknown

27.3 Network: Your family tree can be a money tree.

Relatives are a rich resource of referrals and business.

Research your family tree. Share the family tree concept with members of the law firm. And share resources for family tree information. Does that spark any ideas?

Use the info as an excuse to reach out to extended family members and let them know who you are, what you're doing, and that you have excess capacity (the firm can easily accommodate new clients) and wish to provide your special skills with to a few new clients.

Notes / Comments / Action Items:

27.4 Network: Tap into your family's network.

Talk to your parent's friends. Friends of parents like to support each other's kids (whether their 29 or 69).

Retired folks really enjoy giving a boost to the children of friends. Like your Dad's old Army unit, golf buddies, etc.

Or, go to the network pros, your Mom's friends. How many of them know what you do and that you are looking "for a few good clients."

Is your father from France? Join the local French group.

Notes / Comments / Action Items:

Life got more enjoyable once I learned how to enjoy life.

- New Frontiers International Conference Call

27.5 Network: Where do you frequent?

Does the owner of your favorite restaurant or bar know who you are, and what you do? Do those beneficiaries of your hard earned money know that you have room to take on a few more clients?

Notes / Comments / Action Items:

27.6 Network: Go to alumni meetings. Hand out 10 cards.

List all alumni organizations to which you and the firm members can claim membership. Go to alumni gatherings and tell them what's up for you.

Notes / Comments / Action Items:

27.7 Network: Remember, everyone is a source for new business.

Everyone is a possible client or a potential finder. Who comes to mind right now? Write down those names. Contact them. You MUST set aside time each week to do this. You HAVE to keep filling the biz dev pipe.

Notes / Comments / Action Items:

27.8 Network: Grow your business the old fashioned way.

Before the internet, the librarian was the internet.

Ask your local librarian for ideas on how to grow your legal practice. Librarians continue to have special knowledge on multiple business fields and possess superb connecting skills. You'll be amazed at the happy response.

Notes / Comments / Action Items:

**Yesterday is gone.
Tomorrow has not yet come.
We have only today.
Let us begin.**

- Mother Teresa

27.9   Network: Talk to everyone.

Do not miss any opportunity to chat while standing in the grocery line, post office line, ATM line, bus line, taxi line, ticket line, or theatre line.

Practice an enjoyable and polite way to get into your 15 second elevator pitch.

Everyone you speak with is, at most, six degrees of separation from you and new business, and usually only one or two degrees.

So, when you speak with someone, find a way to ask them for business ("Do you have a will or living trust?"), a business referral, or a referral to someone who might be a good source of business referrals. Give them your card inside the clear plastic business-card-sized envelope that holds the FREE Starbucks coffee card.

Sound successful while asking, "I've just cleared up a couple of matters (or, "I have expanded my firm's resources") and now have excess capacity, do you know of anyone who might benefit from some legal advice?"

Notes / Comments / Action Items:

27.10 Network: Ask your clients for business referrals.

People liked to be asked. "I also wanted to mention that our firm has some unused capacity and would appreciate any ideas, suggestions or new business. I know you don't have a list of 10 referrals right now for me, and, of course, I would be grateful to see a big smile on the MP's face."

Notes / Comments / Action Items:

Continuous improvement is better than delayed perfection.

- Mark Twain

28.1 Eat to win: Have a six figure lunch.

Ask a retired legal marketing director, Chief Marketing Officer, of a major law firm how they were able to grow their firm's business. Ask how they secured their biggest clients.

Ask the LMA for a list of retired CMOs.

You may just walk away with a six figure lead.

Notes / Comments / Action Items:

28.2 Eat to win: Take a retired successful lawyer to lunch.

Retired lawyers need to eat, too. Over lunch they just might share some of their ideas, skills, and enormous list of contacts. Retirement hasn't retired their business development brain. It's still working.

Praise them for their years of excellent service in the field and then ask them how you can learn from all of their experience. Don't be surprised if they give you an idea or two that will help grow your business. See Way #1 above.

People will respect you for respecting them enough to ask.

Does one of your attorneys need a mentor in that retired lawyer's field of expertise?

And there's more than one retired lawyer in your field of interest.

Notes / Comments / Action Items:

Rise above the storm and you will find the sunshine.

- Mario Fernandez

28.2   Eat to win: Take legal professors to lunch -- from your law school and from other law schools.

Which professors are teaching a course that you'd love to pick their brain about? How have some of the professors' graduates grown their businesses?

Write a few names / schools down now.

Notes / Comments / Action Items:

28.3   Eat to win: Take a retired politician to lunch.

Senators, Congressmen, State Legislators, Mayors, Council members. These folks are the preeminent network pros in your community. They have contacts galore!

And they have to eat.

Some prefer breakfast meetings, or a short drink after 5. Whatever their pleasure.

See Way #1 above titled, "Take a retired Judge to lunch." Make the get together about them, their life, their contributions, and their favorite experiences. Any favorite pet projects or charities? Their favorite lawyers and why? Ask them how they think you can serve the community while still having a successful business.

During your meeting focus on them, their interests, and their legacy. What is important to them now? Are there any causes they are currently supporting? Practice the rapport skills mentioned in the neuroscience research, NSR, section and body of science coming out of neurolinguistic programming, NLP. Locate "Rapport, Establishing" in the book's Index or website. Practice "deep listening." Look up "Deep Listening" in the book's Index or website.

Notes / Comments / Action Items:

Being defeated is often only a temporary condition. Giving up is what makes it permanent.

- Marilyn vos Savant

29.1 Work the VAKOG: Always, always have something sweet and FREE in your reception area.

Neuroscience research, NSR, tells us that we enjoy the world (or not) through our control center receptors, the visual (V), auditory (A), kinesthetic (K), olfactory (O) and gustatory (G) senses. VAKOG.

To be desirable you need to send pleasure to as many of the VAKOG senses as possible, as often as possible.

Mints and chocolates will land deep in the sub-conscious pleasure zone. Certainly bottled water, tea and coffee will please many people. Also, small bite-sized low sugar snacks like wrapped single serving packets of saltines, or graham crackers, which will take the edge off a hungry stomach, or help one of many people fighting low blood sugar.

And, if possible, have a few FREE coupons handy.

Provide a two-for-one FREE meal coupon to new clients when they come to your office. Talk to at least three of your favorite restaurants. One of them will have a slow period they need to boost, and will happily provide you with a "Buy One Get One Free" coupon. If you can locate a restaurant next to a theatre, create a package "Special" with the restaurant and theatre.

Notes / Comments / Action Items:

Practice yourself in little things, and thence proceed to greater.

- Epictetus

29.2 Work the VAKOG: FREE lattes.

Provide a FREE latte card at your office to all NEW visitors, new clients and new prospects. Or cut a deal with a favorite restaurant / café /coffee shop and offer a free latte.

You have a "Happy Cascade." The client is happy with you. The café owner is happy with you.

Explore if the café owner can give you the coffee lattes at below cost in exchange for the free publicity received from your firm's promotion to your clients and visitors.

And create a win win TRIPLE R with the café owner. Give the café owner business card sets, a plastic pocket holder that contains your firm's business card along with a 1/2 price latte card good at their café. The "sets" only go to people who own a business and want to be on the firm's e-newsletter email list, or have a legal matter about which they need legal consultation. Your firm agrees to pay the café owner some amount above half price but less than full price for every coupon card turned in.

Notes / Comments / Action Items:

Hold yourself responsible for a higher standard than anyone else expects of you. Never excuse yourself.

- Henry Ward Beecher

29.3   **Work the VAKOG: Chocolate.**

Link your name to chocolate. Become known as the source for really good chocolate!

At the office. At client meetings. Always have chocolate.

Send chocolate along with a "Thank You" note. Send chocolate on birthdays and anniversaries.

Pavlov was right.

When you think of the sweet taste of chocolate, who or what do you think of? Seriously stop and close your eyes. What or who, do you have linked up to chocolate? To me it was a triple-decker chocolate cake when I was a child.

So, become the new "link" to a person's chocolate experience. Chocolate comes in neat little gift boxes. Something as simple as, "I discovered this new chocolate from Switzerland, made from organic cocoa beans, and had to share it with you. Save a bite for your sweetie. You'll score big points! Enjoy!-David." Literally, short and sweet.

Who doesn't want a small box of really great chocolate? It won't be long before a client will say, "Hey, Dave, you brought me some of your great chocolate, right?" That "brain link" operates at many levels including the most primal one. The primal one operates at just below conscious level, just where you want to be. You cannot get a better idea than one that stimulates your desired relationship on the primal level. And do this before your competitor does. For really great organic chocolate mailed anywhere in the world, go to

www.100WaysToGrowAThrivingLawPractice.com/ GreatChocolate in Resource Links.

Notes / Comments / Action Items:

Let me tell you the secret that has led me to my goal. My strength lies solely in my tenacity.

- Louis Pasteur

30.1 FREE. Give something of value for FREE.

There's a reason why "free" is the most popular word in the English language.

When someone has made the trek to your office for the first time besides offering them coffee and a sweet, (come on, you already know Pavlovian reinforcement works consciously and sub-consciously), give them something to take back to their office or home. Give them two free coffee mugs with the firm's website on it, two company ball point pens, and a small box of chocolate in a nice small carry away bag.

With every bite of the firm's chocolate, with every use of the firm's pen, and with every drink from the firm's coffee cup, who pops in to their conscious and /or unconscious mind? The firm!

Do you know how many millions of dollars Nike spends to try and get to someone's brain for 30 seconds? Your cost: some chocolate, a pen and a coffee cup.

For more on the benefit the firm receives by linking a pleasant physical taste sensation to the thought of your firm go to www.100WaysToGrowAThrivingLawPractice.com/ articles and SuccessThroughNeuroScience.

Notes / Comments / Action Items:

Our greatest glory consists not in never falling, but in rising every time we fall.

- Oliver Goldsmith

30.2 FREE: Give a FREE gift that keeps on selling you.

Do you wear glasses? Does the firm have clients and business contacts who wear glasses?

My optical shop puts their card in a small plastic envelope that holds an eyeglass cleaner cloth from Hoya and the optical shop's business card. Brilliant. I asked for three, one for my briefcase, home and car. For low cost eyeglass cleaners and clear plastic business-card sized holders go to

www.100WaysToGrowAThrivingLawPractice.com/ Resource Links _ EyeglassCases.

Notes / Comments / Action Items:

30.3 FREE: GreenFree. Give the eco gift that keeps giving.

FREE. If you're a "green" business, emphasize that fact by giving clients and prospects a solar powered calculator with your name and contact information on it.

To locate a perfect green calculator to promote your firm go to:
www.100WaysToGrowAThrivingLawPractice.com/ Resource Links _ Solar Calculators.

Notes / Comments / Action Items:

I like the dreams of the future better than the history of the past.

- Patrick Henry

30.4   FREE: FREE to you. FREE to your client.

At no cost to you, find a café or restaurant that will offer a special discount coupon for you to hand out. If there's real value there, it's a win win for both businesses. Examples: "a two-for", two meals for the price of one, two lattes for the price of one, two Happy Hour drinks for the price of one, or a "FREE DESSERT" with every two meals purchased. Just ask your favorite restaurant for their ideas. They'll have a few.

Will all parties, meal customers and restaurant owners, think about you and your business when they cash in the coupon? You bet they will! Pavlov meets 5th Ave marketing.

Notes / Comments / Action Items:

**Commitment
leads to action.
Action brings your
dream closer.**

- Marcia Wieder

30.5 FREE: Secure ongoing FREE advertising by going into the clothing business.

Give away a FREE t-shirt at a booth, at a race, in the office lobby, at local gyms, at aerobics centers. Receive free advertising for years and years.

This author still wears a great workout t-shirt with a big ad for a mortgage company. The back of the shirt says, "We give 125%." This free advertising for the mortgage company has been going on for at least five years and is on display for about four hours a week at Gold's Gym.

Create a great t-shirt to wear in the gym for men and women. Don't hesitate to come up with a great catch phrase to put on the back, so that when they're riding the bike, or when they're working out, people behind them will see it.

Create a t-shirt, attractive tennis shirt, wrist sweat band, or something that people wear that gives you free advertising.

For promotional clothing ideas, go to "Clothing" at www.100WaysToGrowAThrivingLawPractice.com/ Resource Links _ Advertising Ideas _ Clothing.

Notes / Comments / Action Items:

Failure
teaches success.

- Japanese saying

30.6   FREE: Give away something free.

FREE. It's worth repeating. Give something that continues to promote your business to that recipient and to that recipient's friends and visitors.

When they do come to your firm, give them something free to take home that has your name on it along with phone number, address, email and website.

Examples: desk top calendar, countertop business card holder, business card holder for a purse or wallet (burnished silver, gold, aluminum for their business cards with your contact information engraved on the back).

Create and print a wall calendar (and /or desk top calendar) of picturesque local places, key community sites, or local events. Many of the directors of boards overseeing those sites and events will want a copy of that calendar for their home or office. For fast, low cost quality calendar printing, go to a local printer who will happily have a TRIPLE R Ranch discussion with you or go to www.100WaysToGrowAThrivingLawPractice.com/ Resource Links _ Printers.

Make sure it is something with your name, website and phone number on it. For ideas, look around your house and office and ask yourself, "Who got me to hang onto something with another company's business name on it?" Do the same thing or go them one better.

Give clients and prospective clients a ruler with your logo on it. Add a phrase like, "Let the rule of law serve you through _____ (fill in the blank) law firm" with your web address, address, email and phone number.

Everyone likes to have a small tin of mints in their pocket, purse, briefcase or desk. Your reception area should have a crystal bowl full of these mint tins with your name on each.

Notes / Comments / Action Items:

**If your actions
inspire others
to dream more,
learn more,
do more and
become more,
you are a leader.**

- John Quincy Adams

31. Hire a marketing employee and receive many FREE promo ideas during the interview process.

Hire a Chief Marketing Officer, CMO. Hire a marketing agent. Hire a marketing firm. Many prospective employees will provide you with FREE research on your target audience to secure your goodwill and employment. Interview at least 5 prospective employees, and notice how much smarter you become in how to build your business. They will provide you with FREE market research, FREE marketing ideas that have worked in the past, and probably a few new ideas, FREE.

And what did it cost you to conduct the interviews? Zero.

If you cannot afford a full time employee, then hire a sub-contractor on a paid-as-used basis.

Just the interview process alone will provide tremendous value to you. Value that will pay for this book by more than 100 times. 1 times = 100% ROI. 10 times = 1,000% ROI. 100 times = 10,000% ROI.

Simply interview 4 marketing firms and you will be at least 200% smarter about marketing your business. If you can afford one of the 4, great, because now you'll bring in your added marketing knowledge gained during the interview process, which will improve the services you receive from the hired firm. In every scenario your business is better for having gone through the marketing firm interview process. If you cannot afford to hire one of the firms, tell them that. It's possible that one of the 4 will be convinced they can grow your business and take the job on a pay-based-on-results basis.

For a list of marketing firms go to www.100WaysToGrowAThrivingLawPractice.com/ Resource Links _ MarketingFirms.

Notes / Comments / Action Items:

Your imagination is your preview of life's coming attractions.

- Albert Einstein

32. Borrow good ideas.

Follow this time-honored tradition.

Whenever you see a lawyer's name in the news, ask yourself, "Is there some way to replicate what they did, or some version of what they did, and generate some news for myself?"

Or read what worked in another city for another lawyer and ask yourself if that can work for you in your city. Be creative and come up with a version of what they did that's different enough to make yours "new" or "newsworthy" in your town. Or wait 6 to 12 months and do the exact same thing.

Notes / Comments / Action Items:

The ultimate measure of a man is not where he stands in moments of comfort, but where he stands at times of challenge and controversy.

- Martin Luther King, Jr.

33. Interview political campaign managers.

Interview or hire a political campaign manager. These folks eat, drink, and breathe promotion. They have garnered great media contacts. More importantly, the good ones know who has the money and what motivates them to part with it. Interview various political campaign directors for their business contacts and "awareness campaign" strategies.

Notes / Comments / Action Items:

Some may suggest that there are a limited number of ways to develop an impressive professional reputation. They're wrong. There are an infinite number of ways to develop an impressive professional reputation.

- Anon

34. Make "seconds" your new first.

Ask a politician who came in a close second out to lunch.

Most will appreciate "winning" your attention as they just fell out of the limelight. If you catch them just after the election, some will have a void now in their life as they were keeping their calendar open for the political position.

After some safe small talk, ask them, "What would you like to do now?" If the answer is a little vague, give them something to do. Hire them, or hire them on a contingency fee basis. Maybe you can give them a part-time networking business development job. Flat fee, or per introduction, or per new client, or some combination thereof.

Hire a "successful" politician who came in a few votes shy of first place. That person may be available for work as a part-time consultant on how to promote your business. Ask them how they could apply some of their "awareness campaign" strategies, promo ideas, and community contacts (group, individual, media) to your business. And what specific advice would they give you to get your firm "elected" by potential clients. They most probably have debt to retire and would welcome a (tax deductible) contribution to their campaign.

Don't forget to say, "I voted for you," if you can.

Notes / Comments / Action Items:

It is good to rub and polish our brain against that of others.

- Montaigne

35. **Interview 5 freelance press release writers.**

If they each share 3 ideas, you know have 15 new ideas.

Freelance press release writers are a unique subset of freelance writers. These are extremely savvy folks as to the requirements essential to appease the appetite of an editor with a sharp pencil, who in turn has a tough boss, hard deadlines, strict content restrictions, and a very demanding audience.

Ask them what kind of story they might write which would help your business grow.

You'll notice that with each new interview, you are a smarter interviewer who can better enunciate your desires and better coax out fresh imaginative ideas from each subsequent interviewee.

Hire one of the writers. Pay any writer whose idea you want to use or embellish upon. Remember these articles become elements of your printed collateral material and helpful additions to your website.

Another unique subset of the freelance writing community are business book ghost writers. Interview three business book ghost writers and you'll hear the creative wheels turning.

For a resource of freelance press release writers or freelance business book writers, go to

www.100WaysToGrowAThrivingLawPractice.com/ Resource Links _ FreelanceWriters

Notes / Comments / Action Items:

My words fly up,
my thoughts remain below:
Words without thoughts, never
to heaven go.

- William Shakespeare
Hamlet. Act III. Sc. 3

36.1 Survey: Bite the bullet and do a client satisfaction survey.

Make sure all the questions you need answered are presented.

Understand your product. Understand your market. Do a survey on how your law practice is perceived.

Before you actually start the survey, list your expected outcomes. Compare your expectations to actual results.

It's never too soon or too late to ask past and current clients these questions:

How did you hear about our firm? Why did you choose our firm over others? What is / was their level of satisfaction with the firm's services? Would they use the firm again for other issues?

Catalog these answers for regular review.

This can be over lunch so you have eye contact when the client responds. [See eye movement behavior during key communication in the NLP section of the book's website, as it is too detailed to review here.] Do not do this over the phone. Better yet, after confirming client's willingness to receive the comment form, send a survey that does not ask for any sender info and is placed in a pre-paid, pre-addressed envelope. The client needs to feel free to "speak his/her mind".

For a good sample survey question list designed by a Fortune 500 Company go to www.100WaysToGrowAThrivingLawPractice.com/ Resource Links _ Client Survey

Notes / Comments / Action Items:

Kind words are the music of the world.

- F. W. Faber

36.2 Survey: Conduct a client satisfaction survey: Part 2.

Use internal resources to conduct a client survey poll, or hire a professional polling service, or contact your local college or university statistics professor. Ask the professor to offer a statistical survey assignment to one or more students as a confidential project and the report will go to you under your name, but the professor and student agree that the student's formal paper will use a fictitious name designation of the firm. A win win.

The client is not told a written survey response is anonymous unless, in fact, it will be anonymous.

You should know that some groups mailing out a written survey form actually place an undetectable change on the return envelope. For example, a font change in the firm's send-to address can tell the recipient exactly who the envelope is from.

Upon receipt and review, the Managing Partner decides on a strategy and meets with the lawyer(s) that work with that client and / or clients of that type. The client manager could then meet with that client and other clients of that type, and say that "at least one of our clients had a response of 'x', and although we hope this was not one of your issues, the firm is nevertheless instituting some firm-wide changes that we hope will benefit you, as well."

Informal client feedback opportunities should be ongoing and certainly taken at the completion of every project and periodically during longer term projects. You never know when a simple, "How are we doing?" can prevent a mole hill from turning into a mountain.

Notes / Comments / Action Items:

Good, the more communicated, more abundant grows.

- John Milton

37.1 Enhance or change your reputation.

Who are you? Who are you to the outside world? Do you like it? Are you satisfied with it? Are you unhappy with it? Change your reputation with a few well-placed ads, articles, event sponsorships, charity fundraisers, etc. Preferably do this after a survey, so you have better base data and a foundation on which to measure a follow-up survey twelve to eighteen months down the road.

Notes / Comments / Action Items:

37.2 Enhance or change your reputation: Purchase a few well-placed ads, articles, event sponsorships, and charity fundraisers.

Preferably do this after a survey of your firm's reputation (see "Survey" in book Index). That way, you'll have better base data, a foundation on which to measure a second follow-up survey twelve months down the road.

Notes / Comments / Action Items:

The first ingredient in conversation is truth: the next good sense; the third, good humor; and the fourth wit.

- Sir William Temple

38. Don't let your fingers do the walking.

Good judgment says don't have a conference call with people that are important to your business, if there is any way you can meet with them personally.

People do business with people they like. It's easier to like you if you're looking into each others' faces.

Notes / Comments / Action Items:

Hear the meaning within the word.

- William Shakespeare

39.1 Get people beating a trail to your door.

Open your conference room to a charity's board of directors.

Get them to come in your front door. Open your lobby to charity events if possible.

Many charities are always looking for a free space to hold an event, a wine tasting, an auction, an art sale, etc. Does your office or building have space that can be used to increase your awareness and improve your image?

If the charity has their own conf room, then, make yours a catered event with finger sandwiches and small desserts to pull them from their conference room to yours.

For every person who somehow finds a reason to walk in your front door, they will have told 1 to 10 people where they are going and why. Later, they'll tell folks why they've been to your office and what they're impression was. Do the math. 100 individuals tell 1 person equals 200 people total. 100 individuals tell 10 people, equals 1,100 people total.

Given the choice between two law firms, people will take the one they "know," have been to, or heard about from a trusted friend, or heard about in connection with a highly respected event.

Get people to beat a trail to your door.

Get people to beat a path to your front door. Open your lobby to charitable events, if possible.

Notes / Comments / Action Items:

People do the best they can with the resources they have.

- Neuroscience Research

39.2 Get people beating a trail to your door: Part Two.

Get them to come in your front door when it is not scary and does not cost them anything, e.g. a free lecture on new tax laws or a promotional fundraiser for a charitable event. Then it will be easier to call your firm when it's going to cost them money or when they have a sensitive scary issue to discuss.

The folds and neurons within their brains are now more "comfortable" with your firm because they've been there and they know you better.

Odds are that every person who somehow finds a reason to walk in your front door will have told 1 to 10 people where they are going and why, or why they've been to your office and what they're impression was.

Get people tracking to your office lobby.

Do the math. 100 individuals tell 1 person equals 200 people (100 + 100). 100 individuals tell 10 people, equals 1,100 people (100 + 1000), etc.

Given the choice between two law firms, people will take the one they "know," been to, or have heard about from a trusted source.

Now that an individual has been to your office they know you better.

The folds and neurons within an individual's brain that has been to your office are now more "comfortable" with your firm because of the law of "familiarity." See book's website for expanded discussion of this law.

Notes / Comments / Action Items:

The law of requisite variety says the person with the most choices, resources and options will inevitably win out over the person with fewer choices, resources and options. So, our job is to ever increase our choices, resources and options within a given circumstance.

- Neuroscience Research

40. Let art attract new clients.

Turn your lobby and reception area into an art gallery.

Change the art every three to six months.

Give the artist an "opening" reception between 5:30pm to 7:30pm.

The artist will talk up your offices for three months or more, and now all the artist's "A" list will know who and where you are.

And be sure to always invite the local media.

The media may surprise you and cover the event.

Notes / Comments / Action Items:

The human species is always motivated by IPO, intended positive outcome, even when it's not consciously obvious.
Find the IPO and unlock the motivation that goes
with it.

- Neuroscience Research

41.1 Think Triple R: Invite folks to the Triple R Ranch.

Reciprocal Referral Relationships. Triple R works.

Take someone from another profession to lunch. Just say, "We have many clients who ask for referrals to other businesses. Maybe we can send some business your way someday."

Most professionals are quick studies and can appreciate what you are saying and would be happy to do the same for your practice.

These are strictly voluntary and not quid pro quo.

If, for example, they are a quality printer, and amongst other finished products, they print a beautiful annual calendar listing all the key holidays and primary holy days along with very nice images for each month.

If, in this example, you are an attorney serving this community, then you might consider providing a link on your website to this very beautiful annual calendar which happens to have the printer's name and phone on every month.

This will garner you great goodwill with that very well connected printer, and provide a service to your firm and website visitors.

Guess which firm will always be mentioned by this printer when the subject of "do you know a good lawyer" comes up?

Notes / Comments / Action Items:

Arguing with a fool proves there are two.

- Doris M. Smith

41.2 Think Triple R: reciprocal referral relationships.

Offer to put newspaper articles about other professionals in your waiting area, and in your newsletter, and ask if they can do likewise in their waiting rooms.

Notes / Comments / Action Items:

41.3 Think Triple R: Contact every major CPA firm in your area.

Your initial purpose: interview them as to their domestic and foreign tax law expertise. You are going to need to "refer complex domestic and foreign tax matters to a CPA firm we can feel comfortable with, along with other accounting issues that may arise with current and future clients."

During the call, you casually insert why your services are uniquely better than others in the following practice areas:

"Possibly we can help each other. Do you ever have clients that have legal needs in the areas in which our firm specializes?" You probably won't say Triple R, reciprocal referral relationship, but everyone can read between the lines.

Notes / Comments / Action Items:

Success in life, in anything, depends upon the number of persons that one can make himself agreeable to.

- Thomas Carlyle

41.4 Think Triple R: Contact a local hotel business owner.

Ask the hotel owner how someone in your business could help them promote their business.   And visa versa.

Triple R. Reciprocal Referral Relationship.

 The "Triple R" business development formula.

He or she just might offer you a free seminar room if the hotel could have a small food and drink concession.

Win win.

Or, start sending your out-of-town guests there in exchange for a special discount.

And say, "By the way, I'm just curious, who handles your legal work for your business and family?"

Notes / Comments / Action Items:

Never part without loving words to think of during your absence. It may be that you will not meet again in this life.

- Jean Paul Richter

42. Find cross-promote relationships.

Find non-competitive companies that would benefit with a cross-promotion.

Insurance brokers and financial advisors are two.

I'll show you mine if you'll show me yours.

I'm referring to email and mail lists with another non-competitive business that would like to speak to your audience, and vice versa.

You can send a newsletter to their mail list, or run an ad, or special interest article in their company's periodic mailed newsletter, or email newsletter, and vice versa.

Kare Anderson is a world class master on this subject.

For more information on Kare Anderson and partnering with non-competitive businesses, go to www.100WaysToGrowAThrivingLawPractice.com/ Partnering

Notes / Comments / Action Items:

The soul of conversation is sympathy.

- Thomas Campbell

43. Hire the top marketing director from a competitive firm.

This is for firms who do not have the good fortune of already having a CMO, Chief Marketing Officer.

Notes / Comments / Action Items:

If evil be said of thee, and if it
be true, correct thyself;
if it be a lie,
laugh at it.

- Epictetus

44.1 No harm in asking: Ask everyone you speak with, "If you were in charge of growing my business, what would you do?"

People like to "rise" to the occasion and will surprise themselves (and you) with some of the good ideas they'll come up with to grow your business.

Ask your waiter and be prepared to increase the tip.

Notes / Comments / Action Items:

44.2 No harm in asking: Bond with people who hire attorneys.

This is so obvious, right?

But are you doing the obvious?

Are you going out of your way to do what is obviously in your best interest? Really?

Notes / Comments / Action Items:

The surest way not to fail is to determine to succeed.

-Sheridan

45.1 Think Press: Become the "go-to expert" quoted by the media.

Notify the media of the your expertise and availability on a moment's notice to comment on related news items. Let all media know you are the "go to" expert on "x."

Let all of your local media, newspaper, radio, and TV know that when it comes to "x" you are the area's leading expert. Ask them for their national contacts, so, you can do the same with them.

At a minimum, go to your town paper and introduce yourself to the editor and publisher. They'll appreciate it, and they have contacts!

Notes / Comments / Action Items:

45. 2 Think Press: Create an on-camera video of you being interviewed on your subject of expertise.

Make it short and newsy, like a real TV news item. One minute max, and end with a lead-in teaser, "...after the break, we'll ask Attorney Franco about the amazing legislation he helped draft."

Then send each media person an email with a link to your video.

Notes / Comments / Action Items:

Insanity is doing the same thing over and over again and expecting different results.

- Albert Einstein

45. 3 Think Press: Issue a press release.

Look for any excuse to link your services or comments with a news event.

Think about everything that you do as a potential press release. And then turn some of those into an actual press release.

Call the media and offer to comment on any news item at all related to your legal field.

Notes / Comments / Action Items:

45. 4 Think Press: Seize opportunities to secure press by doing good.

A recent news story gave a lot of coverage about these hikers hiking for a charity. It would have been nice if the article went on to say that the law firm of Best, Brilliant and Kind were sponsoring their hiking supplies. In this case, it was a Sarah Baldo article about "four combat-wounded soldiers seek to challenge themselves and inspire others by climbing Mount McKinley."

Notes / Comments / Action Items:

Change the way you look at things and the things you look at change.

- Dr. Wayne Dyer

45. 5 Think Press: Become the "expert" in your field.

This seems obvious. Do it because it is.

Again, become "the expert" in your field!

Or, declare yourself the expert and inform all media.

And even if you know there are others who probably know more than you do in a particular sub-set of your practice area that does not mean you hold back from contacting the media and letting them know you are an expert in "x" legal field.

And when you appear on camera or on a radio sound bite you adopt the "as if" mental frame. You act as if you have all the attributes of the smartest person in the universe on the subject and act that way; and you do this the proper amount of humility, and with the appropriate qualifying phrases to cover your assets. The "as if" frame sends a positive message to your conscious and subconscious while at the same time it maximizes your resourcefulness and cognitive abilities.

Notes / Comments / Action Items:

Those who bring
sunshine into the lives of others
cannot keep it from themselves.

- J. Barrie

46.1 Press on: Cultivate relationships with the press.

Always seek out the media desk at a conference and get cards from as many as you can with a promise to call them with anything that may be worthy of their news media. Be sure to ask them what kind of news items they are looking for, and a promise to contact them if you come across anything that fits.

Notes / Comments / Action Items:

46.2 Press on: Do something that merits an award.

Receive an award. Then publicize that fact.

Examples:

Attorney _____ was awarded the _____ Community Service Award, Attorney _____ was awarded the _____ Bar Association Public Service Award, or the _____ Humanities Award, or the _____ Ecology Award, or the _____ Humanitarian Award, or the Boys and Girls Club Good Citizen Award, or the _____ Award.

Find someone to give you an award for something, and then publicize that fact.

Better to say "Attorney" in front of the first and last name, rather than just first and last name. "Attorney" is a public relations statement.

Do something that deserves and leads to an award. Some organizations are not aware they are in a position to give you a Community Service Award, should they choose to acknowledge your kind support of them. List 5 award ideas you can come up with now.

Notes / Comments / Action Items:

By one definition of physics you are the center of the universe. Act like it.

- Ancient Tree

46.3   Press on: Insert yourself into the news.

Ask yourself, "What is getting publicity in my town?"

And then ask yourself, "How do I do insert myself into that news?"

Notes / Comments / Action Items:

46.4   Press on: Save the planet.

Do something in your area that demonstrates your eco-consciousness, your green consciousness. Plant a tree in a local park.

Sponsor a garden at your local _____ (school, university, hospital, nursing home, senior center).

Be presidential. If a garden is good enough for the White House, it's good enough for you. Sponsor a garden and be open to allowing them to give you a plaque on-site that mentions your name.

Anything that lowers carbon emissions will gain favor with many.

Mother Teresa started with _____ and now millions know her name.

Notes / Comments / Action Items:

Better keep yourself clean and bright; you are the window through which you must see the world.

- George Bernard Shaw

47.1 Network like a pro: Join LinkedIn.com.

Don't be short-sighted. Some LinkedIn members have already grown their professional business-oriented list into hundreds of let-me-know-what-I-can-do-for-you LinkedIn contacts. Everyone on LinkedIn knows the primary purpose is to grow one's business. And just like CNN, Fox, and the White House, you too, should consider a presence on Facebook and Twitter. There are other networks that your old pals and past alumni are members of, as well. Be smart like them. Join them. Of course only the ones where you have to give permission before anyone can access your link. You'll be pleasantly surprised who says "hello". There is a reason a Chinese investor paid $100 million for 2% of Facebook. Network as if the business depends on it, because it does.

Notes / Comments / Action Items:

47.2 Network like a pro: Join Facebook.

Why do you think Facebook is so popular? Why do you think a Chinese company paid $100 Million for 2% equity in Facebook? This makes Facebook worth many billions of dollars.

Keep your data minimal and business oriented. All social network sites are subject to hackers and spammers, but not enough for you to forego the many business opportunities therein.

Notes / Comments / Action Items:

Never look down on a person unless you are helping him up.

- Jesse Jackson

47.3   Network like a pro: Tweet, if you can.

The White House, CNN, the City of San Francisco, and 311, all use Twitter.

Is each attorney registered on LinkedIn, Facebook, and Twitter?

I'm not saying spend a lot of time on these sites, but you must be registered, because someone out there will say, "Hey, it's my ol' friend _____, I'll just let him know I'm alive and wish him well." And that person knows 100 people, any one of whom might desperately need your legal services but did not know until now who to reach out to. Now they can reach out to you and bring you business. That's your single and sole purpose for letting a select number of folks know you're alive and well and "open for business."

Do NOT succumb to the temptations of useless "tweets" and worthless "comments". Keep it simple and businesslike. The posture is you're busy but you do have room for a few new clients and would welcome any referrals.

Suck it up and get current with the real world and maybe get one jump ahead of your older, stuffier competition.

The Obama administration sent Tweets in multiple languages for the President's 2009 Cairo Speech.

Notes / Comments / Action Items:

47.4   Network like a pro: BLOG

You must be aware of at least one hot legal blog that you are looking at daily or regularly. Join that blog. Or create an even better one.

Notes / Comments / Action Items:

Interestingly enough
when you become a better
person others want to be
around you and do
business with you.

- Ancient Tree

48. Flex your E-Power with an e-zine.

The business must have an e-zine.

Today, in order to compete, and to compete for "mind space" you must have a monthly e-newsletter.

Start a monthly "Did-you-know" e-newsletter email distribution list. For three good models of interesting and entertaining e-newsletters, go to "E-Newsletters" at www.100WaysToGrowAThrivingLawPractice.com/ Resource Links E-NewsLetterSamples.

E-zine every month. Impress your clients at least once a month by sending them your e-zine (AKA your email newsletter) even if it's just an article you've referenced from your legal newspaper, lawyer magazine, or law review (give credit to the source as necessary). One successful e-zine format is to start with humor, then put the news and/or article, and then end with humor. The best daily newsletter I have seen uses this format: humor, news, humor.

Offer a monthly email on "Legal Issues of Interest," or "Know Your Rights," or Legal Advice You Can Use," or Legal News & Tips" to families and businesses.

You've got plenty of resources to draw from. Use those resources to make you the go-to expert and the top-of-mind attorney for most, if not all, of your e-news recipients.

Notes / Comments / Action Items:

We can escape the prison of our own beliefs and enter the Palace of Possibilities when we allow ourselves to be astonished by everything.

- Gary Craig

49.   Become the out-sourced legal arm of small to medium sized businesses.

Chambers of Commerce and others provide lists of businesses by size (revenue, employee) in any given geo area.

Consider giving these new clients permission to call you "in-house counsel".

Notes / Comments / Action Items:

He who hesitates is lost.

- Proverb

50. Do something worthy of a YouTube.com video in your area of expertise.

Give the video a catchy name, as in, "Sex with the high powered can cause great excitement and great harm."

Cite all the legal problems that could ensue.

Names like Clinton, Sanford, and Woods come to mind.

List three YouTube video ideas, now.

Notes / Comments / Action Items:

Nothing will ever be attempted if all possible objections must first be overcome.

- Samuel Johnson

51.1   Business Card Combo: Try the David King Keller business card + gift card combo idea.

Locate a business card sized translucent plastic pocket holder just large enough to hold your business card and a Starbucks gift card which are the size of credit card.

You can find these plastic pockets on the internet, or simply go to www.100WaysToGrowAThrivingLawPractice.com/ Resource Links _ Plastic Pockets.

Every office supply store sells three ring binder plastic sheets that hold ten business card plastic pocket holders. In a pinch you can cut these up into single pockets, or have an assistant do this.

First ask the potential recipient if they would like a FREE Starbucks Gift Card. A number of folks will not be interested in a FREE $5 Starbucks card, in which case you ask if they would the gift to give to a coffee drinking friend. Those that accept the FREE $5 Starbucks card tucked in a plastic holder with your business card in it will remember you.

When they go home or back to their office, they will separate your card from all the others, and will keep it with them, or in their car till they get to Starbucks, and then think of you again as they pull out the Starbucks card. After using it they will have a "balance" and will save the Starbucks card, and think of you, yet again, when they use the balance on their next latte.

You'll be surprised how many times you will go to "top of mind," or be near the surface of consciousness until that Starbucks card is used up.

See business card + gift card Part 2 on next facing page.

Notes / Comments / Action Items:

Fortune favors the brave.

- Publius Terence

51.2 Business Card Combo: Try the David King Keller business card + gift card combo idea. Part Two.

Use the business card + FREE gift to leverage human behavior science, combining Pavlov and neuroscience research, both conscious and subliminal.

You will now activate and associate two of the best mental triggers in our brains: the olfactory (O) and gustatory (G), a unique combo to add to the visual (V) and auditory (A) and kinesthetic (K) (touch-handshake) experience, VAK. Now you have that magic grand slam home run, the full VAKOG memory stimulation. Go to the book's website and read the section on Neurolinguistics and "Using Neuroscience to Build Rapport and Motivate People." Use those tools and techniques to make it easier for people to accept you, and hire you.

Laughing is a huge VAK hit with many positive associations, and the perfect time to make a nuanced, semi-hypnotic statement. You'll now notice when others do that.

A FREE gift card may be a free parking ticket for your building, or a free pass to a museum that you support, or a local cinema. Come up with something FREE to combine with your card.

For individuals and small business owners, maybe you combine your business card with a separate business card that says, "Good For One Free Hour of Legal Consultation" with your name, address, phone, email, and website printed in a small font size underneath those words. Even though you have said it verbally, there is something about "Good For One Free Legal Consultation" being printed on a card that will literally force most of the recipients to hang on to that card with a mental note as to where they placed it.

Notes / Comments / Action Items:

Where there is love, there is life.

- Mahatma Gandhi

51.3 Business Card Combo: Give away something FREE when you hand out your contact information.

This is an important expansion on the previous Way.

Everyone gives away a business card. Do that and go one better. Put your card in a business card sized see-thru plastic holder that includes a Starbucks free latte card. Your business card will now stand out from the crowd.

Let's say the Starbucks' card has a $5 credit. If their latte costs $3.75, then they may use that card twice. Who are they going to think about for a few precious moments? You! Or they may use the $1.25 balance to help pay for a friend's Frappucinno. The odds are very good that the two of them will spend 15 seconds saying, "What a nice gift from (your name and firm's name)."

In a sense, you just took them out for a cup of coffee in order to, once again, introduce yourself and hand them your card. That was a very inexpensive "top of mind" moment. Ask any ad exec.

If they don't go to Starbucks suggest they use your Starbucks gift as a gift to one of their clients or as a thank you gift for their mailperson, paper delivery person, barber, hairdresser, etc.

Notes / Comments / Action Items:

Our greatest glory is not in never falling, but in rising every time we fall.

- Confucius

52. Make informal interview calls to a list of sub-contractor attorneys.

Tell them you do not have a specific assignment at the moment but are putting together a list of attorney resources.

Ask them about their experience, etc.

As part of the call, make it very clear that you reward lawyers for any referrals.

The call puts your firm solidly in their mind, and when they have a client "too big" for them, who are they going to call to get help?

Triple R.

Notes / Comments / Action Items:

We are still masters of our fate. We are still captains of our souls.

- Winston Churchill

53.1 Affiliate: Do business with other law firms.

Create affiliate law firm relationships in other Cities, Counties, States and other Countries that will allow your firm to provide and advertise expanded services to your clients and prospects.

Create a mutual right to terminate the affiliation for any reason, since you don't know them that well and they don't know you that well. The termination clause will make it easier for both parties to come together. As will a mutual indemnification agreement against a liability caused by the other. And verification that appropriate insurance policies are in full force and effect.

These affiliate offices now have the potential to send you business.

This benefits both firms by demonstrating an expanded national and international capacity.

Ask your tax accountant if these relationships can help you write-off all, or part, of your trips to those countries as business deductible expenses, while visiting an affiliate firm, or researching new affiliate firm prospects.

Connect with firms around the globe and offer to be their contact in your State for incorporation of other services. If they accept, you may be able to say that your law firm has affiliate offices in various other States, and in various other countries, e.g. England, France, Germany, Spain, Russia, Kenya, San Palo, Mexico, etc. etc.

Notes / Comments / Action Items:

53.2 Affiliate: Merge firms.

Merge divisions. Merge practices.

Notes / Comments / Action Items:

Constant dripping hollows out a stone.

- Lucretius

53.3 Affiliate: Contact law firms in your area that do not offer your particular service.

Certainly, most sole practitioners and many small to mid-size firms may not offer your practice area specialty (ies). Paying you a smaller-than-billed fee will help keep the work coming back to you.

There is no reason why the other firm can't continue to retain and control their client, bill the client, and simply reimburse you for the services you are providing out of their total proceeds.

Notes / Comments / Action Items:

53.4 Affiliate: What you can't do can help you.

Not being able to offer a particular legal service is an opportunity. What legal work do people need that you cannot offer?

Make a list in column one of what you cannot do. In a second column make a list of firms that can do those things you cannot do. Highlight the firms in column two that do not do what you do. Then call those highlighted firms and set up a "reciprocal referral relationship." The "Triple R" business development model.

Notes / Comments / Action Items:

Take calculated risks. That is quite different from being rash.

- George S. Patton

54.1　Advertise! Who? Where?

Target audience(s) identified?

What are your target clients reading? Listening to? Watching?

Even a small ad in a publication is read by someone. Those "someones" add up. At some point one of them will need a lawyer. Research the ad's audience. What is the total ad readership? What are the demographics of the readers of the ad?

Notes / Comments / Action Items:

54.2　Advertise! Improve on what the competition is doing.

What's your competition doing? How can you go them one better? Conduct either laser-focused or broad-based advertising. The latest is "behavioral targeting" where someone looking up wills and trusts on Yahoo, for example, can have an ad for your estate services "pushed" to their computer screen when they go back online. For narrow demographic marketing techniques, go to www.100WaysToGrowAThrivingLawPractice.com/ article _Lazer Marketing.

Notes / Comments / Action Items:

Love builds bridges where there are none.

- R. H. Delaney

55. Go green.

Go eco. Go _____-friendly (fill in the blank).

Issue a press release that Your Law Firm has gone green.

You might get lucky, hit a slow news day and get coverage.

Notes / Comments / Action Items:

To improve status quo you must change status quo.

- Ancient Tree

56.1 Sponsor a benefit lunch: in honor of a retired or retiring judge.

Others will kick themselves for not thinking of it first.

You'll garner prestige within the legal world, and a much heightened awareness by the press and media. One of a dozen media will pick up on the story.

Be sure to have a quotable media sound bite that honors the judge from you, as well as a quote from the judge honoring his past experience in service to the community.

The retiring judge just might take a liking to you and you just might gain a lifetime of contacts.

Notes / Comments / Action Items:

56.2 Sponsor a benefit lunch: in honor of a retired or retiring politician.

See the Way just preceding this one.

Politicians can have a whole different set of contacts than judges. This opportunity will allow introductions up and down the political spectrum along with their various organizational structures.

Very importantly, who were the large financial backers of these politicians? These folks have legal needs for their financial resources as do those with whom they regularly communicate. It is these you most want to invite, and meet with, at the luncheon.

Notes / Comments / Action Items:

We are all motivated by a keen desire for praise, and the better a man is, the more he is inspired to glory.

- Cicero

56.3   Sponsor a benefit lunch: for a local or national icon.

For a beloved and respected person, living or deceased. With proceeds going to that person's family or favorite charity.

You can honor national icons like Mother Teresa and MLK, or a local celebrity who is dearly beloved by the community who is either alive or dead.

Any size practice can do this. The smaller the firm, the less the firm can underwrite the costs, and therefore the more the event ticket reservation costs. For the right honoree and guest speaker(s) the larger the audience, and increased chances of media coverage.

Notes / Comments / Action Items:

They can because they think they can.

- Virgil

57. Contact the 50 largest condo boards, and Home Owners' Associations (HOAs) in your area.

Who is their attorney?

Are they happy with current legal representation?

Who do they know that could use a good law firm?

Yacht club boards need lawyers.

Have a partner and junior associate assigned to each Board.

The associate can sit for the partner as needed.

Remind the associate that all members of a Board, and their business associations, are prospects for new business, and that every encounter with the Board should be approached from that point of view.

Notes / Comments / Action Items:

Success is the sum of small efforts, repeated day in and day out.

- Robert Collier

58. Have a pop-chocolate quiz.

Periodically, ask someone in the firm for a description of the firm's services.

A good answer is rewarded with very high quality chocolate. :)

Notes / Comments / Action Items:

The greatest results in life
are usually attained by
simple means and the
exercise of ordinary qualities.
These may for the most part be
summed in these two:
common-sense and
perseverance.

- Owen Feltham

59.   Offer to sponsor the printing of an event's brochure.

Allow the event's organizers to give you a "Thank You" note on the brochure.

Notes / Comments / Action Items:

60.   Donate legal time to a charitable auction.

Make sure many of the bidders looking at the auction list are your prospective clients.

Or, donate one free estate and will planning session, or one free hour of legal consultation.

Notes / Comments / Action Items:

61.   Coach a Little League team.

No reason why you can't have some fun and network at the same time.

Notes / Comments / Action Items:

Failures do what is tension relieving, while winners do what is goal achieving.

- Dennis Waitley

62.1   Connect: with the well connected.

Become an advisor to the Mayor or City Council member in your area.

What council member couldn't use a little free legal advice? That person will know many of the movers and shakers in the immediate area you might wish to meet. And they will know many of the local Judges, as well. Try and guess how many times a year someone will ask them, "Do you know a good attorney....?"

Notes / Comments / Action Items:

62.2   Connect: Be social.

Attend social functions where you will be seen by clients and prospective clients.

Warren Buffett allows his photo to be taken playing bridge for a reason.

Yes, it can be a pain to get up and out, but the clients are out there, not in your office or home. And most of the time you come home saying you were glad you made the effort.

Exhibit A: list all successful attorneys who are reclusive?

Notes / Comments / Action Items:

The difference between a successful person and others is not a lack of strength, not a lack of knowledge, but rather a lack in will.

- Vince Lombardi

62.3   Connect: Go where the business people go to meet.

Restaurants. Clubs. Athletic facilities. Resorts. Who owns that space? These owners are speaking with business people every day. Some of those folks / businesses need a lawyer from time to time. Set up a Triple R (reciprocal referral relationship). "I'll try and steer business your way, in addition to referring friends and other businesses to your establishment. I can also handle your legal issues and arrange for some form of discount. And I can accumulate free legal time for your benefit for any business referrals you send my way."

Notes / Comments / Action Items:

62.4   Connect: Each firm member should be involved with at least one local charity.

At a minimum each firm member has introduced himself to the head of a charity's board. In how many charitable functions does the firm participate?

Notes / Comments / Action Items:

62.5   Connect: Take up a sport that forms relationships.

Golf anyone? Bridge? Go climb a mountain, run a marathon, sail, etc.

Hang out with high achievers. List a few:

Notes / Comments / Action Items:

I cannot give you the
formula for success,
but I can give you the formula
for failure -- which is:
Try to please everybody.

- Herbert Bayard Swope

63.1   Join: a community organization. Where? Who?

Notes / Comments / Action Items:

63.2   Join: a few impressive organizations.

At the age of 27 this author became a member of ATLA, The American Trial Lawyers Association. At the time the author was hiring various lawyers and needed access to ATLA resources. List a few of the organizations you've been thinking about joining.

Notes / Comments / Action Items:

63.3   Join: a club frequented by prospective clients.

List the clubs which would maximize potential client contact. Get one or more firm members in every key club.

Notes / Comments / Action Items:

Fears, of various types, are the biggest impediment to making a request for a business transaction, aka a sale.

- Ancient Tree

64.1 Lead and connect: Become a Board member.

Many for profit and non-profit boards would welcome an attorney on their Board. Maybe the understanding is that any advice you can provide at a meeting is free. But any advice that requires research, or 9 to 5 time, will have to be billed out, but at a greatly discounted rate. Many attorneys simply attend Board meetings for groups who have their firm on retainer. It comes with the retainer package.

Source your inner Captain James T. Kirk.

Notes / Comments / Action Items:

64.2 Lead and connect: Join a community organization.

Join a non-profit organization.

Try and add something like this to your resume: Attorney _____ is on the Board of _____. (Dance Theater, School for _____, YMCA, Guide Dogs For The Blind, Corstone, Meals On Wheels, etc.) What would impress your target client base? Which non-profit has the largest, wealthiest support base consisting of potential clients or people that could introduce you to clients?

Consider your club, school, church, etc.

Notes / Comments / Action Items:

It's always too early to quit.

-Norman Vincent Peale

It's never too early to quit the wrong activity.

- Ancient Tree

65.1 Join a legal org: e.g. become an officer of your local legal association.

Lawyers refer business to lawyers, just like your doctor refers you to other doctors.

Notes / Comments / Action Items:

65.2 Join a legal org: e.g. become a committee member the national bar association.

Some committee examples? Average time required? Benefits? See National Bar Association website.

Notes / Comments / Action Items:

65.3 Join a legal org: e.g. become a committee member of a State or County court advisory and rule making commission.

Establish close working relationships with judges.

Notes / Comments / Action Items:

Success does not consist in never making blunders, but in never making the same one a second time.

- Josh Billings

66.1 Go to Chamber of Commerce business-to-business Mixers.

Chambers specialize in providing speed-networking opportunities. If your Chamber doesn't offer it, recommend it.

Speed-networking is like going to a cocktail party, but you don't wander randomly from person to person. In this case, you are only talking to people who want to talk business development. So you won't get "stuck" with someone who goes into a 30 minute story "trance" about Uncle Harry's medical malpractice law suit, and you've lost all that network time to meet someone who might actually bring you business, or become your next great running / golf / sailing / bridge partner. This process guarantees you won't spend more than 5 minutes in front of someone. Yet, if you sense a synergy or opportunity, you make a note to contact them later.

When networking, remember, in many cases, it's not the person in front of you who will do business with you; it's the person they know and refer to you because you made a positive impression on them.

And realize you are only going for just one or two good connections. So, be polite, extremely polite, when speaking with that 95% you wish they were someplace else other than in front of you. You never know when a frog will turn into a princess, or, has a cousin that is your perfect prince.

Notes / Comments / Action Items:

**Trust your intuition.
It will provide you with thoughts
flashes of insight, and
'messages' which are
creative, playful,
and sometimes
bizarre.**

- Cherie Carter-Scott

66.2   Go to Chamber of Commerce business-to-business mixers.

If you are a sole practitioner, or want to give an associate a little marketing practice, take advantage of the many Chamber of Commerce B2B, Business To Business, events.

One chamber in San Rafael, CA sponsors "The 5 minute speed-networking event."

It's a little like speed dating, but different.

Two people are allowed to interact for only 5 minutes, about 2 1/2 minutes per person. You exchange cards and elevator pitches. Those that wish to will follow up with the other.

Example: The Chamber allows 20 business people to register. There is a fee for hosting, organizing, coordinating location, etc, about $25. 20 business people gather, 10 on each side of a long conference table (or 3 tables u-shaped). People are assigned random numbers 1 A - 10 A, and 1 B to 10 B; 1A sits across from 1 B, the moderator starts the session, and after 5 minutes, a gong is hit, and the "B's" all shift 1 seat to the right while the "A's" remain seated. Now 1A and 2B are sitting across from each other and have 5 minutes to introduce themselves and their business to the other.

Notes / Comments / Action Items:

There are no passengers on spaceship earth. We are all crew.

- Marshall McLuhan

67.   Know thyself.

Do you know what might be holding you or other firm members back from being an even better Rainmaker? Some challenges are conscious. Other challenges are on the edge of consciousness and can be easily brought to one's attention and effectively addressed in a short amount of time with the right coach who is a master in neurolinguistic science. Some of this research is 30 years old, and reinforced by recent studies done at Stanford. Some of it is touched upon by Don Goewey's book, Mystic Cool, The Neuroscience of Success. Goewey cites numerous studies on how to wire the brain for success. Don't be fooled by the word "mystic". It alludes to studies done with the Dalai Lama's monks who have an uncanny, yet easily explained, ability to remain incredible calm (cool) in the face of great stress as recorded by studies done at the University of Wisconsin. Under lab conditions, these monks have a startle response rate that is, remarkably, lower than members of the U.S. President's Secret Service Team. For a link to the "instant calm button" go to www.100WaysToGrowAThrivingLawPractice.com/ articles _Instant Calm

Goewey's website says: "What if, in doing just one thing, you could rewire your brain to deliver: 1) an immunity to [unhealthy] stress, 2) the flow of creative intelligence that turns work into the joy of excelling, 3) the emotional resilience to be positive, peaceful and confident, 4) the social intelligence to love passionately and compassionately, and 5) the mind-body connection to sustain the energy and health needed to succeed. All of the above are neural networks generated by a healthy brain." For a link to Mystic Cool go to: www.100WaysToGrowAThrivingLawPractice.com/ Resource Links _ Mystic Cool

Notes / Comments / Action Items:

When I read drinking was bad for you, I stopped reading.

- Henny Youngman

68.　Win with humor.

Successful people know how to make you smile. They weren't born with it. They developed it.

Take a lesson from Carol Bartz, CEO. In a New York Times interview she confided that she won't hire a new executive unless she has experienced some humor in them in their initial meeting.

Memorize 5 good jokes. Come on, you can do it. You like to laugh, right? So does everyone else.

I know where you can hire a famous $10,000/hour comic writer for FREE. Record the opening monologues of Letterman, and Leno. Pick one good joke a night and practice sharing it with one person a day. That way your material is always fresh and you can "blame" it on Leno, if it falls flat.

Most people don't stay up that late watching TV. Watch the previous nights recorded monologue over dinner the next day.

Research shortcut: ask to get on author's FREE humor email list that will include jokes from folks like Letterman, Leno, Conan O'Brien, etc. Go to www.100WaysToGrowAThrivingLawPractice.com/ Resource Links _Humor Email List.

Notes / Comments / Action Items:

I strive to be as good a person as my dog thinks I am.

- Anon

69.1 Relax: Have more fun.

Have more fun with people doing what you like to do: playing bridge, swimming, bowling, riding horses, playing tennis, hiking, running, team rowing, . . .

You'll radiate "I'm fun to be around, and fun to work with as your lawyer."

Notes / Comments / Action Items:

69.2 Relax: Write, read, pray, meditate . . .

People who can quiet their mind a few minutes a day seem to derive benefits.

Notes / Comments / Action Items:

70. Don't buy into any advice about limits.

Don't buy into any advice about "limits" of what you can or will achieve.

Notes / Comments / Action Items:

The ability to convert ideas to things is the secret to outward success.

- Henry Ward Beecher

71. Write a book on your subject.

Send it to a publisher. Or self-publish. You could self-publish a handful of books for under $1,000.

For self-publishing support, go to www.100WaysToGrowAThrivingLawPractice.com/ article _ Self Publishing.

Wouldn't you like to be introduced as, "Attorney _____, author of (place book title here)."

Ask any publicist. It's a lot easier to promote someone who has written a book in their field.

Notes / Comments / Action Items:

72. Get free on-line time management suggestions / support.

To receive "10 Easy Steps to Recover Time", go to www.100WaysToGrowAThrivingLawPractice.com / articles _ Time Management

Notes / Comments / Action Items:

It's a scientific fact that all new
momentum must begin
by going out of
balance to the
current momentum.

- Ancient Tree

73.1 Speak: Get their attention when you speak.

Blanket your listener with scary stats:

33% of contracts lack an essential element,

45% of teens and adults protesting a parking ticket, or DUI, had a worse result than those same protests represented by an attorney,

33% die without a will and cause havoc, distress and sometimes lawsuits among surviving relatives,

68% of negotiations had better results when represented by an attorney, and

the single best way to delay a decision you WANT to delay is to say, "Let me discuss this with my attorney and I'll get right back to you."

Then you say while smiling, "So, lawyers aren't all bad. They have their bright side."

Then go into your specialty or the topic agreed upon with the meeting organizer that would be of significant interest to the audience.

Notes / Comments / Action Items:

73.2 Speak: to your community.

Give a free talk. Where? To whom? Local community organizations. Lions Club. Rotary. Various Chambers of Commerce in your area. Lunch. Look up clubs and community organizations in yellow pages. The Women's Club, for example. Call City Hall and ask for the names of all registered organizations, or just look in the yellow pages. For some talking points see Way #38.

Notes / Comments / Action Items:

The ability to concentrate and to use your time well is everything if you want to succeed in business -- or almost anywhere else for that matter.

- Lee Iacocca

73.3 Speak: Make two to four public speaking engagements a year.

Do this for each practice area. Make a quick list of topics and audiences now. For any fears or issues about presenting to a group contact the author.

Notes / Comments / Action Items:

73.4 Speak: Give a free talk.

Where? To whom? Local community organizations. Lions. Look up clubs / community orgs in yellow pages. Call your City Hall or Chamber of Commerce and ask for name of all registered orgs. This is great practice for associates.

Notes / Comments / Action Items:

73.5 Speak: Give a lecture at trade shows attended by prospective clients.

What trade shows do firm's clients and prospective clients attend? Be there in a public way.

Notes / Comments / Action Items:

73.6 Speak: Speak somewhere to someone on your topic of expertise.

Give your brain 30 seconds to come up with 2 good examples, right now. Write those down.

Notes / Comments / Action Items:

In everything, the ends well defined are the secret of durable success.

- Victor Cousins

73.7   Speak: to an audience of potential clients.

Find a way to become a speaker and address your colleagues at meetings they attend. Can some smaller or larger firms use your specialty(ies)? How are they going to know about you and your services?

Speaking topics: some stats will help. For non-attorney audiences use stats in Way # 38

Be sure to do a dress rehearsal in front of a friendly, yet constructively critical, audience beforehand befor the actual event.

Educate them on the "Feedback Model" in Way #9.12, and then give your talk.

If you need a speech coach, go to www.100WaysToGrowAThrivingLawPractice.com/ Resource Links _ Speech Coach.

Notes / Comments / Action Items:

73.8   Speak: Beef up resume by speaking at a local university.

Speaking to a class at a local university will allow you to say, "Legal Issues Lecturer at _____ University" in your biographical description, or in your business resume.

When giving a lecture, maximize the publicity value by issuing a press release for the university paper, and local newspaper if the topic is newsworthy enough.

Or, place an "informational ad" in the local newspaper, and with the professor's and the university's permission say "room for 5 guests," call 123-44Me to attend.

Notes / Comments / Action Items:

The desired outcome, clearly defined, becomes the engine that creates achievement.

- Ancient Tree

74.   Attend conferences.

Attend laser-targeted conferences. Specifically, attend the trade conferences that your clients and prospective clients attend.

This is obvious, right? But are you making time for the obvious?

Notes / Comments / Action Items:

75.   Talk to the talkers.

At every conference you ever attend, develop rapport with the presenters. Ask for their business cards. (They won't hesitate. They are also there to promote themselves.)

Stay in touch with all of them. Inevitably you'll need key expert advice which they can quickly provide.

Sometimes a speaker or panel expert will know someone who needs representation in your geographic area and they will think of your firm. Why? You are "top of mind" because of your occasional touch base note, email, or newsletter.

At every trade show, and at every event, be sure to introduce yourself to every speaker. If you miss their presentation due to a conflict, then go to the event's Press and Media Coordinator. They will know where the speakers are, or how to easily reach them. These speakers are consummate networkers.

Notes / Comments / Action Items:

If you don't know where you are going, you'll end up someplace else.

- Yogi Berra

76. Set up a speaking engagement with a well known celebrity or politician.

Arrange for the celebrity to speak at your annual conference. Or sponsor this celebrity speaker at a meeting of your potential clients such as the League of Women Voters, or the U.S. Chamber of Commerce.

Feature your guest speaker at a key lunch break.

A great guest speaker is Robert Ballard. Ballard is famous for finding the Titanic.

Ballard is a fascinating speaker and he and the Titanic become a draw card and part of your lead for press releases.

More interesting, in Ballard's opinion, is that he discovered that life on Earth began earlier than originally thought when he found life in deep water super hot thermals.

Ballard is president and founder of the Institute for Exploration at Mystic Aquarium. Led by Ballard, this institute is focused on the development of a suite of remotely-operated vehicles created specifically to conduct deep-water archaeological excavation.

Ballard has conducted more than 100 deep-sea expeditions during his career and is the recipient of numerous professional awards, including the National Geographic Society's prestigious Hubbard Medal and the National Humanities Medal from the National Endowment for the Humanities.

Another fascinating speaker and a huge audience and media draw card is Sir Richard Branson.

Notes / Comments / Action Items:

No pessimist ever discovered the secret of the stars, or sailed to an uncharted land, or opened a new doorway for the human spirit.

- Helen Keller

77.1 Teach: a class.

Teach a CLE, Continuing Learning Education, course. Where? To whom? This author was an instructor of a marketing course for one semester at the University of California, Berkeley. It was in their Lifelong Learning University Extension Program. There are any number of subjects you could teach that might attract the program director's interest. Contact the Bar and explore a course through the ABA.

Notes / Comments / Action Items:

77.2 Teach: Conduct an evening course.

Or offer a Saturday afternoon seminar. Select subjects important to the public: wills, trusts, tax shelters, IRC 1031 tax deferred exchanges, best practices in property sale and purchase, different ways to take title, etc. etc.

Titles like: "Ten Ways To Use The Law To Save Taxes."

You could do this through your club or church.

Notes / Comments / Action Items:

78. Support groups like Corstone.

Corstone is dedicated to helping people faced with cancer and terminal illnesses.
www.100WaysToGrowAThriving LawPractice.com/ Corstone.
Sponsor a charitable event in the firm's lobby, e.g. a wine auction. For more,
www.100WaysToGrowAThrivingLawPractice.com/ articles _Charities.

Notes / Comments / Action Items:

If you don't know where you are going, any road will get you there.

- Anon

79.   Barter.

Trade $5,000 worth of legal services for $5,000 worth of something you want. How about a trade with the restaurant where you entertain clients?

You can tell the company you're bartering with that they can take pieces of that $5,000 and give it to friends or other business associates. Simply charge your highest possible rate as part of the barter. Experiment with this. It just might bring you in a couple of new clients with billable hours far in excess of the amount you bartered.

Notes / Comments / Action Items:

Life can be pulled by goals just as surely as it can be pushed by drives.

- Viktor Frankl

80.1 Sponsor: a charity's website.

Sponsoring a site isn't all that expensive. A small website with five static pages can be as little as $20 a month. More sophisticated sites with a lot of bells and whistles can run up to $300 / month, more or less, before IT maintenance and design costs. You may already have an IT person who might just contribute some of their free time to support the charity in partnership with the firm. One web hosting company was providing a 5 page website and domain name for under $60 a year. For a low cost web hosting company go to: www.100WaysToGrowAThrivingLawPractice.com/ Resource Links _ Web Hosting.

Select a popular local charity with wealthy and influential board members. Tell them you were thinking about sponsoring the web hosting costs for a charity's website. Just the "hosting" as an ongoing donation, not the cost of any IT staff or any people time required to update the site.

"I'm sure the staff at our firm would love to see just a small acknowledgement when they visit the site. Maybe something on the bottom of the Home Page like,"Website hosting is sponsored by www.BrilliantKindSmart.com, a full service law practice."

Guess how many of the charity's site's visitors will click on your site to find out more about you?

Notes / Comments / Action Items:

Our plans miscarry
because they have no aim.
When a man does not know
what harbor he is making for,
no wind is the right wind.

- Seneca

80.2   Sponsor: or Co-sponsor a charitable event.

Sponsor new artists, art shows, local youth events, sports events. All of these events will generate positive publicity!

What charitable function in the last 9 months have firm members participated in that availed them of an audience greater than 100 people?

Major charitable donors have businesses and family matters that require attorneys. There is no better time to meet someone than at an event demonstrating that you support something for which they have great passion.

Notes / Comments / Action Items:

80.3   Sponsor: a bike race.

Sponsor a run, running group, marathon, walkathon, or spelling bee. Sponsor a fundraiser or a fundraising group at an event, e.g. Race/Walk for a Cure.

Better yet, sponsor an Invent-a-Thon for the idea that best helps improve the community as judged by the retired Mayor, and retired judges. Note the easy, graceful opportunity to contact a few retired judges.

Notes / Comments / Action Items:

If you find yourself in a hole,
the first thing to do is
stop digging.

- Anon

80.4 Sponsor: a children's school play whose parents are potential clients.

Some parents may think, "Your law firm helped my child. I like you more and I know you better now. I trust you more and I'll keep your business in mind."

Again, do it first and foremost just to be a good neighbor.

Find the most expensive grade school or high school in your area and ask the principal what could your firm sponsor... a play perhaps....one where most of the parents will want to attend. The playbill handout would have a cover credit on it stating in a good size font:

Sponsored by
the law firm of
Brilliant, Kind and Thoughtful
www.BrilliantKindThoughtful.com

Notes / Comments / Action Items:

80.5 Sponsor: Girl Scouts, Boy Scouts, Cub Scouts, Life Scouts, Senior Scouts, etc.

Notes / Comments / Action Items:

81. Take an org poll amongst firm members.

Ask for a list of the chambers of commerce, community organizations, charities, clubs and alumni groups with which the firm members are actively involved.

Notes / Comments / Action Items:

Who aims at excellence will be above mediocrity; who aims at mediocrity will be far short of it.

- Burmese saying

82. Establish a "Markies" Night.

Marketing Awards.

You need an Academy Awards night where Oscars are given out for the Best Marketing Idea, The Markies. Best New Client Introduction. Best Introduction of Someone Who Introduced Us To Someone. Best 4th Generation Lead To a New Client. Most Generations Between Lead to New Client and The Firm, The Most Degrees of Separation Award.

Any excuse for a party! Have a "Red Carpet" entrance. Lights! Cameras! Action!

For a more complete list of award titles go to:

www.100WaysToGrowAThrivingLawPractice.com/ articles _ Marketing Oscars.

Make the awards fun and also worthwhile. "And the Markie goes to ...." Give an actual "Oscar" gold-looking Statue, or some fun new design.

Give a dinner for 2 to _____ restaurant (which restaurant has agreed to give you a 2 for 1 special menu dinner for 2 in exchange for a year-long-in-firm promotion and ongoing goodwill of the firm.)

Notes / Comments / Action Items:

**If you want to feel rich,
just count all the things you have
that money can't buy.**

- Anon

83.   Have a "Findies" Award.

Create an award for your "Finders."

You'll be surprised how motivating this will be to some folks.

Check out the reaction of the idea on your mailman, FedEx person, UPS delivery woman, your doctor's receptionist, your dentist, your dental hygienist, and your office maintenance people.

Give "Oscars" to your network of friends who refer new business to you. "And for the BEST New Business Introduction Award, we have dinner for two in Paris, or a weekend at a nearby Resort and Spa, complete with daily massage, manicure, facial, and a Life Time supply of my undying love and gratitude."

These awards are for your NETWORK of finders.

Tell your friends, "Hey, if you introduce our firm to a great client, or introduce us to someone who introduces us to a great client you can win an Oscar, A Finder's Award Oscar Statue, and dinner for 2!"

Ask yourself, "What would I want to be given as a fun incentive to get me to network my friend's business?" Would FREE Starbucks for a year do it? !!!

$5 per day x 365 days = $1,825. $1,825 for an idea or contact that brings in a six figure account is a good trade!

So, you tell everyone the Best Client contact has a prize of Starbucks lattes for a year. If anyone you talk to even calls the firm, the firm will send you a FREE Starbucks card good for 5 FREE lattes!

Everyone has fun, and you win.

Notes / Comments / Action Items:

We choose our joys and
sorrows long before we
experience them.

- Kahlil Gibran

84.1   Get Political.

National Republican and Democratic politics is the most
professional networking opportunity anywhere. Encourage
firm members to get involved with a National political
party on a National, State, or County level. Where's the big
money? In big politics. Who wields the most influence as
in Supreme Court appointments? The White House.
Photos with the President of either party are still photos
with the President of the United States. Should you
sponsor a breakfast for the next incumbent or challenger
running for President? Presidents and Parties never run
out of a need for money.
Help them get some. Gratitude is always good for business.

Get involved 18 to 24 months before the election. That's
when people still have time to meet you, and lower cost
functions will still garner those very close connections.

Notes / Comments / Action Items:

84.2   Get Political: Work with your local County or State U.S. Presidential Election Committee.

By doing this you will meet that party's "A list."

These folks work with the President of the United States.
Does the networking get any better, more serious, or more
loyal? Every four years, firm members have a chance to
get involved in a big way with big ticket players who
remember who worked with them. How many firm
members are involved with U.S. Presidential politics and
election committees? Try to have firm members connected
to both parties.

Notes / Comments / Action Items:

Friendship is the hardest thing in
the world to explain.
It's not something
you learn in school.
But if you haven't learned the
meaning of friendship, you really
haven't learned anything.

- Muhammad Ali

84.3 Get Political: Become a legal advisor to a politician.

This is worth repeating. Become a legal advisor to a political candidate. Scary? Yes. Do they have lots of contacts? Yes.

Notes / Comments / Action Items:

84.4 Get Political: Become an advisor to a U.S. Senator in your State.

The Senator will know virtually every mover and shaker in the State whom you might wish to meet, and a lot of the State and Federal Judges, as well.

Notes / Comments / Action Items:

84.5 Get Political: Become an advisor to your U.S. Congressperson.

Connect with the well connected.

Your Congressperson will know every mover and shaker in the congressional district you might wish to meet, and a lot of the local, State, and Federal Judges, as well.

How? Offer to head up "District # ____
Attorneys-For- _____."

Or, on a smaller scale (with close to the same benefits) offer to head up "(Your Town) Attorneys-For- _____."

They will meet with you and assess your allegiance to their cause and party. And after the proper amount of vetting, you're in.

Try and guess how many times a year someone will ask your Congressperson, "Do you know a good attorney....?"

Notes / Comments / Action Items:

By associating with wise people you will become wise yourself.

- Menander

85.   Run for an office.

Worth repeating. Run for a public office, even if the odds are against a victory.

Careful you don't alienate any important public officials. And minimize, to the extent possible, any reason your opponent should dislike you personally.

Be friendly, say only good things. Virtually every story of the election will mention your name and what you do. Political campaigns generate massive advertising and public relations.

Even if you lose, you win, as long as you've left a positive image with a much larger number of people than when you started your campaign.

Notes / Comments / Action Items:

86.   Support your local District Attorney and State Attorney General.

And make sure they know it. Both probably have committees in support of him or her. Get on one. At a minimum, make a small donation of $50. It will be noticed and appreciated.

Notes / Comments / Action Items:

87.   In some obvious manner, support your local police and law enforcement agencies.

They meet people every day who need a lawyer.

Notes / Comments / Action Items:

You must be the change you wish to see in the world.

- Mahatma Ghandi

88. Send birthday cards to your clients, prospects and friends.

Yes. Spend $2. Buy a real card and personalize it with your real signature. Leave out anything that is not personal to the individual. (Don't stick in a press release.) Make it about them. Say at least one thing that's personal. If you can't say something personal, add a personal touch with a fun quote.

Or, sound smart and cute by borrowing this Irish toast, "May the worst days of your future be better than the best days of your past."

Email is only a back-up to the real deal. If you've missed the mailing deadline and the birthday is today by all means send an email. Wait 30 days then send the press release. "Hope your birthday was the best. Here's what I've (my firm has) been up to. P.S. "There's always room for more business, and any of your good biz dev ideas."

Notes / Comments / Action Items:

89. Fix a building.

Homeless shelter. Retirement home. Veterans meeting hall. Etc. And allow them to put up a small, but visible, plaque when the improvements are done along with a dedication photo op for the local press. Which building comes to mind?

Notes / Comments / Action Items:

If two individuals get together and exchange a dollar, they each walk away with one dollar. If the same individuals get together and exchange an idea, they both walk away with two ideas.

- Thomas Jefferson

90.1 Practice Area Research: Ask a Social Studies class to do a study on one of your practice areas.

If you like the results, issue a press release on the study.

Do this as a class project, or as a thesis, or a case study by an individual student. One option: focusing on who, what, where and when does society need said legal practice and where and how has society used this aspect of the law.

Suggest that a Social Studies, Economics, Law, Marketing or Advertising class do a study of your services (or one specialty) as a class project. Focus on product / service (practice areas), target audience, and best ways to reach said audience by researching what has worked in the past for others and what could be different in the future to more effectively reach the desired client base, e.g. price points, message, etc.

Notes / Comments / Action Items:

90.2 Practice Area Research: Ask a University Masters, or PhD level, class to study the science and art of marketing professional legal services.

Sponsor a reward for the person or class that comes up with the best three business development ideas, e.g. offer a partial tuition scholarship, a new laptop, a new iPod, etc.

Award a part-time contract to the person with the best idea(s) to grow your business, i.e. hire that student part time upon graduation, to help implement the ideas they came up with.

Notes / Comments / Action Items:

If you spend your life constantly trying to be 'there,' 'here' will never be okay.

-Cherie Carter-Scott

90.3 Practice Area Research: Test new practice areas.

Test new revenue sources with the occasional outreach into new markets.

Notes / Comments / Action Items:

91. Let a law student bring you business.

Invite law students to bring you a client with a legal issue to your firm and inform them they will be temporarily hired as your assistant on the project while receiving law practice experience firsthand.

Not all, but many law students come from families who have some degree of wealth or some degree of influence in their business or community. Sponsor forums at local law schools. Tell them it will beef up their resume and give them an edge over other law school graduates.

Notes / Comments / Action Items:

I hold a doctrine, to which I owe not much, indeed, but all the little I ever had, namely, that with ordinary talent and extraordinary perseverance, all things are attainable.

- Sir T. F. Buxton

92.1 Tap university resources: Ask a university marketing class to adopt your law firm as a project.

Ask the students to come up with 50 ways to grow your business. Sponsor a reward for the person or class that comes up with the best three ways, e.g. offer a partial tuition scholarship, Starbucks Coffee gift cards, dinners for two, free movie tickets, a new laptop, a new ipod, etc.

Which University are you thinking about as you read this?

Notes / Comments / Action Items:

92.2 Tap university resources: Ask a university advertising class to adopt your law firm as a project.

Or, suggest that the professor suggest this idea to one or more of their students as a special project for extra credit.

Do not forget to offer the professor a chit for a FREE exploratory legal consultation for his or her use, or that of a family member or friend.

Notes / Comments / Action Items:

92.3 Tap university resources: Ask a University communications / public relations class to adopt your law firm as a project.

When you come by to discuss who you are, bring a stack of $5 Starbucks cards plus a stack of coupons good for a sandwich at the local café, and a bottle of wine, or box of chocolates for the professor.

Notes / Comments / Action Items:

Obstacles don't have to stop you. If you run into a wall, don't turn around and give up. Figure out how to climb it, go through it, or work around it.

- Michael Jordan

93.   Think "cultural outreach."

What languages do the members of your firm speak? How can you reach out to others who speak those languages? Join organizations and clubs that cater to those cultures / languages.

Encourage lawyers and associates within the firm who have diverse cultural experiences, to promote the firm's business within those various cultural groups. Tell them it might help their personal business development goal of "x" new clients, and "y" new client matters per quarter.

Notes / Comments / Action Items:

94.   Raise your SEO.

Google your area(s) of work. Notice what comes up. Notice who comes up. Notice if your firm comes up. If not, why not? What is the firm's SEO rating, Search Engine Optimization ranking, in each key practice area? Is there a legal treatise on the firm's website for every key practice area that shows up on Google and Bing?

For methods to achieve a top 5 listing in Google search and for more SEO ranking improvement go to 100WaysToGrowAThrivingLawPractice.com/OurSEORanking

Notes / Comments / Action Items:

Patience, persistence and perspiration make an unbeatable combination for success.

- Napoleon Hill

95.1 Web Power: Drive people to your website.

Drive lots of new prospects to your website by placing "goodwill" links on your website.

Create website gold. Build goodwill fast. Place links on your website that will give people important resources and other incentives to visit your website.

Every time someone goes to your website it's the same as them picking up the newspaper and you're the headline story. They're reading about you, thinking about you, yet, you control the story line, a public relations paradise.

Follows are dozens of ways and reasons for hundreds of people, prospects, and referral sources to now come to your website who never would have come otherwise.

The most obvious way to drive folks to your website is with photos of them or people of interest to them. Post photos on your website of the charity event you sponsored, co-sponsored, or were simply connected to in some way. Capture key people, key scenes, and make sure you're in a few.

Most people love to see photos of themselves and of others. The charitable organization will want to see them and download them for their records. The charity's board members, key donors, and supporting foundations will also want to see the photos on your firm's website. All of these people will be thinking of your firm for a few minutes or longer as they click on the URL link to your website and begin to view the images from the event. Be sure to have a link back to your firm's home page. Many visitors will decide to browse your site to learn more about you. That's a grand slam home run in the business promotion world!

Notes / Comments / Action Items:

Fall seven times, stand up eight!

- Japanese proverb

95.2   Web Power: Drive people to your website: Part Two.

When posting photo links of interest to your website, do so quickly.

Get the photos up to your site fast with emails going out the very next day with the link to your website. Send a few key images you select to the press that night. You might get lucky with a blurb in the morning paper. Some of the attendees will have their own PR agents who may forward the images of their client to their neighborhood paper, or to the City's monthly magazine that caters to their social set and will always run a few images of events about town, especially charitable events.

If possible, get a photo of your firm's name in the images somehow, e.g. photo showing name of the firm at door's entrance if held at your location. Or a close-up of the event brochure with the firm's name clearly legible, so that as folks scan the images, the firm's name will clearly stand out for a second.

Send everyone you can an email with a link to the photos on your website. Don't forget to send a link to your local papers, weeklies, and monthly magazines.

Example: For photos of our Christmas / Holiday charity fundraiser go to:
www.MyFirmName.com/PhotosHolidayCharityEvent

How many wealthy people and significant clients are now going to your website who never would have gone otherwise? How many friends and relatives wanting to show off their latest images (and do-good-ness) will send people to your website? How many will inevitably discuss what kind of law the firm practices?

Notes / Comments / Action Items:

The person interested in success
has to learn to view failure as a
healthy, inevitable part of the
process of getting
to the top.

- *Dr. Joyce Brothers*

95.3 Web Power: Use photos to drive even more people to your website, your virtual lobby.

Place a link to photos of a little league sporting event on your website. Yes, an international law firm based in New York can easily provide a link for its San Francisco law firm to safely and securely upload this week's Rocket Soccer Team Game Photos. How many moms, dads, uncles, aunts and grandparents will now go to your website who never would have gone otherwise? How many friends and relatives wanting to show off their latest photos of little Jonathan and Maria will send them to their friends? More people coming to your website! How many of these folks need, or know people who need, or work for firms that need, your services?

Maybe one of your lawyers is a little league coach. Great! Link the team's photos to that lawyer's profile. It's simple, safe, and creates great goodwill. Or spend a few dollars and become a co-sponsor, buying the game's bottled water or t-shirts.

Now you have folks beating a path to your virtual door, bringing them much closer to becoming keenly aware of who you are, liking you, browsing your website and thinking of ways to send you business. Many will think, "Anyone who is a friend of little Johnnie is a friend of mine." Others will say, "A firm that supports my little Nancy is a firm I want to support."

Each web link you put on your site is a separate and distinct way to grow your business.

Notes / Comments / Action Items:

The important thing in life is to have great aim and to possess the aptitude and the perseverance to attain it.

- Johann Wolfgang Von Goethe

95.4 Web Power: Add links on your website that contribute to public service.

Have at least one link, and preferably multiple links, that relate to every practice area.

Each web link you put on your site is a separate and distinct way to grow your firm's business.

Create 100 reasons for people to come to your website.

Link up anything you think your clients would be interested in. Come up with reasons for them to look at your site daily. Drive people to your website.

Notes / Comments / Action Items:

95.5 Web Power: Have a "Top 10" drop down button.

Top 10 things to do in preparation for an earthquake, home fire, food poisoning, death, marriage, birth, business merger, hiring an employee, firing an employee, establishing a trust, or in case of a missing child.

All of these should significantly increase your SEO, Search Engine Optimization.

On your website give your clients and prospects a list of web services that will serve their interests and needs, and those of their family. As a reward to you these same people may keep your web address as a preferred site and their first step when needing to locate those resources.

On the "food poisoning" drop down, after you cover all the immediate care aspects, add a note to contact the firm if a third party is responsible for the food poisoning and damages were suffered. Be sure to inform them that one type of food poisoning, Staphylococcus Aureus, can cause fainting while driving at 60 MPH. Ask the author.

Notes / Comments / Action Items:

It's kind of fun to do the impossible.

- Walt Disney

95.6 Web Power: Create links on your website to government sites.

Add any number of links on your website that would be perceived as a public service.

You have more than one office door. You have your literal office door and you have your virtual office door. Get people to beat a path to your virtual office and that will bring them that much closer to your actual office.

Create:

www.MyFirmName.com /Federal GovernmentWebsites
www.MyFirmName.com /State GovernmentWebsites
www.MyFirmName.com /County GovernmentWebsites
www.MyFirmName.com /City GovernmentWebsites

Link your website to a U.S. Federal Government resource site, your State's resource site, your County's resource site, and your City's resource site. And if you're big enough add all States and all Counties.

A few more examples of sites your clients / prospects need to visit on occasion:

www.MyFirmName.com/department of planning
www.MyFirmName.com/Gov/HUD/LoanModProgram
www.MyFirmName.com /my congressional representatives
www.MyFirmName.com /my government.
www.MyFirmName.com /local library
www.MyFirmName.com /USSenators.
www.MyFirmName.com/my us senator representative
www.MyFirmName.com/state's resource site.
www.MyFirmName.com/county's resource site.

Notes / Comments / Action Items:

Love yourself, trust your choices, and everything is possible.

- Cherie Carter-Scott

95.7 Web Power: Become a politician's new best friend.

This next business development opportunity applies to all firms but especially those specializing in government liaison work. Contact every politician for your City, County, and State. Ask them for a profile to put on your website with a web link to their own site. Do the same for department heads. Then establish the link within 24 hours of them sending you that info, and a confirming email back to them with the link asking them if their description is "OK".

Now, every State, County, and City elected official and department head has put their profile on your website.

Don't just provide a link; provide the profile sketch and a link. The profile makes your website "personal" to the politician. How many other websites actually have their photo and profile? It will cause them (force them) to go to your website at least once, if not multiple times, especially when they periodically update their profile.

Many people aware of your site will make that their first stop when needing to contact a government office or department. Guess what website will come up when that official or government office is Googled or Binged? You may not be the first website listed by Google or Bing but your website may be on page one of the links giving the firm a free promotional boost every time. How many government and public service resources can you get on your website? At a minimum, have just one button labeled "Public/Government Resources" and then let the fun and "clicks" begin. How many local news articles or legal publication articles can you attain by announcing this service?

Headline: "Is Smart, Best and Brilliant setting a new public service trend?"

Notes / Comments / Action Items:

In every culture and
in every medical tradition
before ours, healing was
accomplished by
moving energy.

- Albert Szent-Gyorgyi,
Nobel Laureate in Medicine

95.8   Web Power: Drive politicians to your website.

Politicians will be happy to provide you with a short description of themselves for your website along with a link to the official site of their government office.

Now, all of a sudden you're going to double up in their awareness and that's a good thing. Every year, you can say when you see them, "Anything you want me to add to your profile on our website?"

Ask each department head for an example of a "win" that their department accomplished for the City. Add that info to their reference, e.g. "We remove 20 metric tons of trash a day from the City with minimal inconvenience and maximum recycling."

Imagine having those conversations. Imagine how emblazoned your name and your firm's name will be in their mind going forward. Imagine if somebody had done that for you and put your profile on their website. Wouldn't you think about them periodically, or fairly regularly? Once a week? How many times would you check out your photo on the law firm's website?

Those individuals will be happy to provide that information, and suddenly your law firm's profile will increase tenfold in their awareness, and that's a good thing. Ask them, "What is great about you, as a person, as a man (woman), as a professional?"

Did you notice the Triple R (reciprocal referral relationship) opportunities built into the political website links? Triple R leads to the most important "R", ROI.

Example: www.MyFirmName.com/USGov/ SenatorDianneFeinstein.

Notes / Comments / Action Items:

Love is the willingness to be yourself and live in harmony with others.

- Cherie Carter-Scott

95.9 Web Power: Add a Government Chart link to your website.

It's simple enough, but it will attract business people, researchers, poli-sci students, political activists. Now anyone seeking the name and contact info for their government representative might just go to www.MyFirmName.com/Gov/Chart

This will chart all the names from their local rep right on up the chain to go as high as you want: to the Governor, all elected Federal reps, and on up to the President.

www.MyFirmName.com/Gov/StateLocalDepartments

Create your government services web links on your website, and beef up your online marketing by beefing up these website links. Take advantage of this opportunity right now, before your competitor does.

When you (or your assistant, law student, intern, trainee) talk to these City/County/State representatives and Federal representatives for your State, ask them for their photo, profile and mission statement.

Politicians and candidates are networking pros. Gain "access" to politicians in high places. Go to their fund raisers. Go to their websites and check their events calendar. Find a charity you both like. Contact specific politicians and tell them you like their work and will be making a contribution in their name to the mutually admired charity. Win. Win. Win.

If you need help setting up these links, go to your IT department or go to www.100WaysToGrowAThrivingLawPractice.com/ articles _Web Links Set Up.

Notes / Comments / Action Items:

Disclosing builds bridges, withholding builds walls. Your choice: walls or bridges!

- Cherie Carter-Scott

96.1 Web Charities: Create links on your site to charitable organizations.

This will drive even more people to your website, your virtual reception area.

Simply have a drop down link called "Community Services," or "Local Charities." Or provide a link on a specific attorney's profile of a charity he or she supports, e.g. www.MyFirmName.com/AttorneysName/Charity.

Sidebar: requiring an attorney within the firm to be a sponsor becomes a way to gently turn down any charity that does not fit that "sponsored charity" requirement.

P.S. There's nothing wrong with being wooed by a charity. You agree to attend a Board meeting to listen to their community goals and objectives. Most Boards have people on them you want to know. Inevitably, you'll be asked to talk about your firm and its service to the community, which you describe vis a vis all the services you provide within all your various practice areas. Of course, before the meeting you've asked for a Board profile, so, you know with whom you'll be speaking.

Notes / Comments / Action Items:

Love is caring enough to tell the truth.

- Cherie Carter-Scott

96.2   Web Charities: Interview charity's Executive Director before adding their web link to your site.

Tell them you might include their non-profit within your Estate and Tax Planning practice area under your Community Charities List.
Each charity mentioned will provide you with a special three line summary of the charity's mission statement to place on your website with a web link to their site. Simple. Safe. Great public relations. Terrific goodwill. And will most certainly increase traffic and SEO.

Now you might get invited to their events, and you might meet with their Board of Directors. In fact, before placing a link on your site, be sure to ask to speak with their Board President / Chairman.

You might be asked to give a 5 minute presentation on your area of expertise to the Board. This is the same Board that contains wealthy locals, business owners, and fund raisers who continually rub elbows with your clients and potential clients.

The charity's Executive Director will send an email to all Board members, staff, and key contributors telling them of this new development with a link to your website. How many wealthy people and significant clients will now go to your website who never would have gone otherwise? How many will inevitably browse your website and discuss what kind of law the firm practices?

Given a choice of two law firms to select from, one firm with a web link to their favorite charity and one that doesn't, who is going to get first crack at their business? Each charity mentioned will thank you in ways that will bring benefits to your firm for years and years. And what did you do? You put a link on your website.

Notes / Comments / Action Items:

The Athenians,
alarmed at the internal
decay of their Republic,
asked Demosthenes what to do.
His reply: "Do not do what you
are doing now."

- Joseph Ray

97.1 Web Magnets: Create 100 reasons for people to come to your website.

Add links to your website that will attract people to your site. Link up anything you think your clients would be interested in. Come up with reasons for them to look at your website daily. Put them all under one button, if you like. Or a button under a button, e.g. "Community Services," then "More Resources."

All of these websites already exist. Your IT person simply creates a URL link from your website to those websites. Safe. Easy. Fast.

Create links to hook up to other sites. It's all automatic. Your web IT people will know how to do it. Or get easy fast support by going to: "Setting Up WebSite Links" at www.100WaysToGrowAThrivingLawPractice.com/ articles _ Web Links Set Up.

You'll be surprised how many people would just as soon link through your website rather than search it out on their own.

If you could secure just one extra "visitor" a day, that would be great. But with these website links you may get 100's of extra visitors a day, and many of them will forward a link to your website to others. This is viral virtual marketing. Effective. And what did it cost you? Next to nothing. And your marketing went to people you never would have reached otherwise. And some of these emailed links to your website were referrals by friends, the acme of business development marketing.

Don't make the mistake that your firm is too big and too prestigious to provide "resource" links because your competitor won't.

Notes / Comments / Action Items:

Love means establishing clear boundaries rather than building up resentment.

- Cherie Carter-Scott

97.2 Web Magnets: Add web links on your website that capture an even wider spectrum of online visitors.

The following links are typically absolutely free and they're automatically refreshed by professionals:

Examples:

www.MyFirmName.com/DailyLegalTip
www.MyFirmName.com/DailyWisdom
www.MyFirmName.com/DailyWeather
www.MyFirmName.com/CommunityHeadLines
www.MyFirmName.com/SportsScores
www.MyFirmName.com/DailyJoke
www.MyFirmName.com/DailyHealthTip
www.MyFirmName.com/DailyPuzzle
 www.MyFirmName.com/DailyBusinessTip
www.MyFirmName.com/DiscountCoupons
www.MyFirmName.com/RestaurantSpecials
www.MyFirmName.com/ProfessionalServices
www.MyFirmName.com/BankMortgageAndCDRates
www.MyFirmName.com/CriminalDefenseNews
www.MyFirmName.com/HeadlinesNews/CNN/FOX/MSNBC
www.MyFirmName.com/NYTimesLaughLine

Notes / Comments / Action Items:

Trust is an inner knowing
that you can count on yourself
to do what you say you
are going to do.

- Cherie Carter-Scott

97.3 Web Magnets: Add more web links on your website that capture an even wider spectrum of online visitors.

Examples:

www.MyFirmName.com/DailyHumor
www.MyFirmName.com/MortgageRates
www.MyFirmName.com/RealEstatNews
www.MyFirmName.com /weather
 www.MyFirmName.com /Traffic
www.MyFirmName.com /WorldTime
www.MyFirmName.com /free stuff
www.MyFirmName.com /free theatre tickets
www.MyFirmName.com /something free every week
www.MyFirmName.com /local plays
www.MyFirmName.com /local shows
www.MyFirmName.com /local cinema
www.MyFirmName.com /local comedy
www.MyFirmName.com /financial aid
www.MyFirmName.com /educational scholarships
and grants
www.MyFirmName.com /daily puzzle
www.MyFirmName.com /BestOfLists
(get this list from a local / regional magazine)
www.MyFirmName.com /inspiration
(safe, non-controversial messages)
www.MyFirmName.com /daily quiz
(It's like crossword puzzles. People love them and many
are addicted to them. Leverage that love and passion by
bringing them to your site to get their fun fix.)
www.MyFirmName.com /local library reference section

Notes / Comments / Action Items:

Little minds are tamed and subdued by misfortunes; but great minds rise above them.

- Washington Irving

97.4 **Web Magnets: Create 20 more reasons for people to come to your website.**

Have a firm-wide contest for website link ideas with a prize for top 5 entrants both in quality, quantity, and originality. Give those ideas to your website manager and firm's marketing director.

For a step by step process to easily acquire these links for your firm, go to www.100WaysToGrowAThrivingLawPractice.com/ Resource Links _ Website Link Examples

and

www.100WaysToGrowAThrivingLawPractice.com/ article _Web Links Set Up process.

More Examples:

www.MyFirmName.com/ThreeThingsToDoToday (The above activity listing is a very popular feature column in the San Francisco Bay Area's Marin Independent Journal.)

www.MyFirmName.com/TenThingsToDoThis Week
www.MyFirmName.com/311HelpLine
www.MyFirmName.com/LocalJobsWanted
www.MyFirmName.com/LocalJobsAvailable
www.MyFirmName.com/EstatePlanningArticle
www.MyFirmName.com/ForeclosureAvoidanceResources
www.MyFirmName.com/homeRetentionOptions
www.MyFirmNamc.com/YourIdeaHere
www.MyFirmName.com/local library
www.MyFirmName.com/ [add your idea here]

Notes / Comments / Action Items:

The waters wear the stones.

- The Book of Job 14:19

97.5 Web Magnets: Inspire. Through the website offer a daily email with an inspiring quote.

Let people know your daily inspirational quote is available.

Let them know through the firm's e-zine and website.

You'll be surprised how fast that email list will grow, and the occasional great feedback you'll receive. You will now be "top of mind" in the legal world for those folks receiving that daily email. In fact, please include me, David King Keller, in any inspiring emails or e-newsletters at david@KBDAG.com.

If you need a list of inspiring quotes send an email to the author and I will forward same to you.

Notes / Comments / Action Items:

The man who removes a mountain begins by carrying away small stones.

- Chinese proverb

98.1   FREE: Attract Prospects: Establish a website link titled www.MyFirmName.com/FREEStarbucksCard.

Use the Starbucks craze (or latest equivalent) to grow your client prospect base.

YourFirm.com/Free Starbucks coffee. Guess how high that will raise your Search Engine Optimization, SEO?

The "very, very, very narrowly defined" recipients will pay with information, and a sufficient percentage will become clients. Example: To qualify, "You must be over 30, have at least 10 years work experience, and answer 'Yes' to at least one or more of the following questions. Will you be requiring any of the following legal services within the next year: making out a will, a living trust, forming a corporation, a family trust, forming a 501C3 corporation, suing someone, require legal mediation, legal negotiations, require employment or engagement contract review, pre-nuptial agreement, tax counsel, entering into a commercial lease, or other matters requiring legal counsel." You list only those questions the answer to which point to a specific prospect in your practice area(s). Say the responses will be held in the strictest of confidence.

To receive the FREE Starbucks Card good for at least 2 FREE Grande Lattes, they simply fill out the short survey. Capture their email address to instantly confirm they've "Won a FREE Starbucks Gift Card!", their mailing address in order to send the Starbucks GIFT Card, and their phone number to call offering FREE-No-Obligation consultation on next steps for their legal needs. The call is made before sending the Starbucks card to verify address, discuss legal needs and to make sure it's not an 18 year old latte junkie.

For those who don't visit Starbucks, we have a FREE Gift Certificate to Amazon.com (or equivalent). Read 98.2.

Notes / Comments / Action Items:

The first and greatest commandment is, don't let them scare you.

- Elmer Davis

98.2 FREE: Trade Starbucks lattes for business leads.

Recipient must fill out a survey that shows a list of legal services that just happen to coincide with your legal services and those to whom you have an affiliation or referral agreement, and include two blank spaces for "other." Make sure Trust, Will, and end-of-life-directive are on the list.

Then ask the person to, "Check off one or more types of legal services I might need help with in the near future."

"Check off three or more legal services my friends or family might need help with in the near future."

"Check off three or more legal services my business might need help with in the near future."

"Enter your company's web address and your title with the company." Say that submitting the request for a FREE Starbucks card also allows them to FREE Legal Tips email communication from the firm to them with their right to unsubscribe to the emails at any time. State that their information is for legal firm use only and treated as strictly private and confidential. A small percentage will become clients, or refer clients.

Possible scenario: at $2,400 minimum income per client, one client pays for 300 eight dollar Starbucks gift cards! In the short term 75% won't pan out, and 20% will be dead ends. That leaves 5% who use your firm, or refer someone to your firm. Five percent of 300 equals 15 new clients. 15 new clients times $2,400 minimum each in gross revenue equals $36,000. And one of those may become a six figure account. And you now have 300 new people on your monthly e-newsletter. On average, some of those additional names will become clients, or refer a client. It's a web link triple play: come to your web / capture an email address / beat a path to your door.

Notes / Comments / Action Items:

Imagination is more important than knowledge. Knowledge is limited. Imagination encircles the world.

- Albert Einstein

99.1 Web Magic: Have a Community Events Calendar link on your website.

Guess how many "hits" your website will receive when someone Googles (or Bings) "community events?"

Guess how many "hits" your website will receive when all major event planners for key community organizations go to your "Community Events Calendar" web link to double check for an event conflict when considering availability of a specific calendar date?

Call your local paper, Chamber, or Visitor's Bureau and find out who prints or publishes a Community Events Calendar. Once you locate that person, offer to put a link to that calendar on your website. Ask that person how an event planner checks for key community events to avoid a major conflict when appealing to cross-over patrons and attendees? Ask how an approved person is allowed to enter an event on the calendar.

Team up with that Community Events Calendar person, or create your own with the help of your IT specialist and the calendar printer mentioned in the previous Way.

Guess how many people you, or a staff member, can now have an excuse to call because their events have a link on your website? The opera, art festivals, sporting events, etc.

And any IT person can tell you how to make the Community Events Calendar link perfectly safe as to your websites integrity. If no one has a site with a Community Events Calendar for your area, you're in luck. You can set up a separate URL non-interactive site for under $100 a year and upload the calendar to that site with a link from your site. For a little more money, you can create a Community Events Calendar that is interactive with those to whom you give a password. See book Index for Charitable Events Calendar discussion on that subject.

Notes / Comments / Action Items:

Energy and persistence conquer all things.

- Benjamin Franklin

99.2 Web Magic: Place a "must visit" Charitable Events Calendar link on the firm's website.

Has the firm considered the website-visit-client-conversion-ratio and enormous ongoing goodwill with wealthy 501C3 board members, by placing a "Charitable Events Calendar" link on the firm's website?

When a charity intends to plan an event whose website will they check to avoid any date conflict with another charity? The firm's? Radical? Not really. It's easy to do, and don't be the second firm to offer this to the well established charities in your area.

Not just any charity. Only charities that are well established, well liked, and are non-controversial. Tell any charity you don't want to list, that a member of the law firm must be a sponsor and involved with them.

Tell IT that, of course, you want to make it easy for charities to update the calendar, so IT builds a wall, or better, simply a link to a separate URL website. So, a charity is given a password to that separate URL (and doesn't come anywhere near the firm's website). Therefore, there is no risk to the firm's site. But for all appearances, the link originates from and is part of the firm's site.

Can you estimate how many wealthy folks and charities will be coming to the firm's site? Your IT specialist can track the number of "hits" that are related to this link. Once the link and Calendar and update mechanism is established with "log-in rights" granted to every registered, approved and sponsored charity, send an email out to all approved charities stating that the link is active. Guess who else will check your link? Big social event planners for weddings, plays and symphonies will check your website. Make sure every professional event planner is sent a link.

Notes / Comments / Action Items:

**Dost thou love life,
then do not squander time,
for that's the stuff life
is made of.**

- Benjamin Franklin

100. Interview 12 companies that need to make you money to secure your business.

The sales and advertising departments of various media must sell you on their ability to add net revenue to your bottom line in order to win your business.

Remember "top down". Start with asking for the President of the media or the SVP in charge of sales or advertising. These are going to be your most senior and most experienced parties who may have ten more years experience over the regional sales rep in charge of your territory or vertical market. In order to win your business each advertising or sales exec will give you multiple examples of what they have done for other law firms (free ideas for you!) and three to five examples of what they can do for your firm specifically. More FREE ideas for you!

Interview 3 newspaper advertising departments, 3 regional or national magazine advertising departments, 3 radio station advertising departments, and 3 website companies whose sites are frequented by prospective clients and feature "ad windows." If you receive three ideas from each one, then you just gathered 3 ideas from 12 sources for a total of 36 potentially new and innovative ideas to grow your business.

And what did it cost you to conduct the interviews? Zero.

If you can afford one or more of the promotional budgets, great, because now you'll be able to supplement the strategy with the hired firm with all the other ideas you generated. If you cannot afford to hire any of the firms "until our business grows," tell them that. It's possible that one of the 12 firms is so convinced of their ability to grow your business that they will allow your firm to pay on a based-on-results basis. Websites can charge on a click-through-only basis assuring you that the visitor actually clicked over to your firm's website.

Notes / Comments / Action Items:

What would life be if we had no courage to attempt anything?

- Vincent van Gogh

FREE.

25 More Ways FREE right now.

Simply go to the book's website.

www.100WaysToGrowAThrivingLawPractice.com

Click the "More Ways" tab.

Our doubts are traitors, and make us lose the good we oft might win, by fearing to attempt.

- William Shakespeare

FREE.

36 More Ways sent to you via monthly email.

Enjoy the stimulation of a monthly business development strategy sent to your Inbox at the beginning of every month.
Simply go to the book's website.

www.100WaysToGrowAThrivingLawPractice.com

Click the "More Ways" tab, and when you fill in the email info form for the FREE 10 MORE WAYS, just check the box labeled: "Please email me the Free Monthly Biz Dev Tip".

Your information is kept strictly private and confidential.

We usually don't make change when we see the light, but when we feel the heat.

- K. L. Murry

FREE.

A unique, low cost, lifetime gift for clients.

For a unique gift idea that the author will only share with one law firm in each major metro area email David@KBDAG.com and place "100 Ways _Unique Gift" in the subject line.

For more Ways to grow your business go to www.100WaysToGrowAThrivingLawPractice.com

or email the author at

David@KBDAG.com

Executive Coaching ROI

How does executive coaching give me a return on my investment?

Executive consulting/coaching is already a big trend in corporate America. According to Fortune magazine, it has developed as one of the hottest management tools in recent years. "It is a grassroots movement that is spreading in some of the unlikeliest corners of corporate America, including IBM, AT&T, and Kodak." No small wonder. A recent study about executive coaching for a Fortune 500 firm by MetrixGlobal reported, "a 529% return on investment and significant intangible benefits to the business."

Support for a similar high level of ROI is found in other consulting/coaching studies. And the use of executive coaching does not appear to be "a flash in the pan." A recent 2006 study about coaching in Fast Company [Online] states, "63% of organizations say they plan to increase their use of coaching over the next five years. Most telling, 92% of leaders being coached say they plan to use a coach again. Both indicate strong endorsements of coaching; the first by the organizations paying the bills, and the second by the leaders who are actually receiving coaching."

For multiple studies and statistical research on the ROI of executive coaching for yourself and lawyers in the firm, go to www.100WaysToGrowAThrivingLawPractice.com articles _ ROI of Executive Coaching.

Executive coaching arrives at law firms

Law firms in the United States have not ignored this coaching phenomenon and are beginning to use coaches more strategically. In a 2006 story in The Recorder, Northern California's leading legal newspaper, one commentator says:

> "But as coaches become a more commonplace fixture in American law firms, their roles are becoming more structured. Some firms have begun formal coaching programs for associates and junior partners to navigate the thorny transition from service lawyer to business getter. Others have brought in coaches to help their most senior leadership deal with issues as vital as client retention and as solemn as succession planning."

Coaching is also making an appearance on international law management radar screens. For example, in June 2006, Ark Group, a leading British legal consulting firm and publisher of Managing Partner magazine, produced a full two-day seminar in London, UK on Coaching for Law Firms: Making it work! The Ark Group puts forward the following rationale for the conference:

> "With clear evidence that executive and performance coaching is producing tangible organizational and individual benefits in a wide range of sectors, there is clearly accelerating interest within many legal practices to explore and invest in coaching and mentoring."

The growth of coaching within law firms is fuelled by the recognition that many lawyers in developing their management and marketing skills respond more positively to one-to-one/small group-based coaching than to team/large group-based learning."

Executive coaching arrives at law firms (cont)

All lawyers in the firm, regardless of current level of performance, should see coaching as a means to take them to a higher level of success than they can achieve on their own. Coaching will make what is good in their practice -- even better. Sound coaching is designed to grow people's strengths and develop their individual talents. To draw an analogy, most professional athletes would never dream of competing without the assistance of a coach who will stretch them to attain peak performance. Why wouldn't lawyers want the same advantage?

And in today's competitive environment, coaching is growing to become a critical part of building and maintaining a thriving legal practice. As one director of business development at an AMLaw100 San Francisco firm stated, "This has gotten quite popular...my own take is that... everybody is looking for an edge, an advantage."

◇◇◇

What Is Your Practice Area Rating?

Use the following scale in your rating:

*¹Skill Level Rating Scale:

0 = wish to be in this area but no one in the firm with this skill yet;
1 = minimal skill;
9 = best in your geo area (multi-city firms list practice area by city; 9.5 = best in your geo area is generally agreed to by other lawyers and legal writers in that geo area;
10 = best in this practice nationally;
10.5 = best in this practice nationally / internationally is generally agreed to by other lawyers, legal writers, and law professors.

*2 Practice Area's PR Rating to Target Market:

Add up the points:
0 = No publicity;
1 = Practice Area is in brochure;
1 = Practice Area on website;
2 = Speak /Lecture in this Practice Area;
2 = Train/Teach for CLE;
3 = You have Published Articles in Practice Area;
4 = Media about you in this area written by others;
5 = Publicly Honored with Award in this area;
6 = Book in this area;
_ = Other (you rate relative to above).

Example: If the practice area is in the firm brochure, on website, and you've lectured as well as published an article within that practice area = 1+1+2+3 = 7 points total.

PRACTICE AREA RATING TABLE

100WaysToGrowAThrivingLawPractice.com

	Specific Practice Area	Skill Level 0 to 10[*1]	Practice Area's PR Rating to Target Market 0 to 10[*2]	Are There Ways To Improve Practice Area: Yes / No	Action To Be Taken
1					
2					
3					
4					
5					
6					
7					
8					
9					
10					
11					
12					
13					
14					
15					

The Art and Science of Selling

Follows is a very brief overview culminated from decades of professional sales training, both given and received. More information is available on the book's website.

First, don't listen to people who tell you selling is difficult. Is that the message you want running through your brain every time you approach a sales opportunity? No.

Anyone can sell.

To successfully sell you only need two things: motivation and technique.

Listen to people who can help you make selling easier, a lot easier. Selling becomes much easier than many other things a lawyer does during the course of a year when the techniques of selling are broken down into individually customized, easy-to-process, bite-sized pieces.

Again, it's not the "selling" that's hard. What's challenging is finding out what to do, and then, making the time to do it. That is, once you are sufficiently motivated.

You have to have both, M&T, motivation and technique.

First, you must have motivation. A good business development coach skilled in neuroscience research, neurolinguistic programming, executive coaching skills and the real world of law firm practice can help establish motivation and incentive, both internal and external.

Second, you must have technique. The firm member must be trained in various proven business development techniques used to secure prospects, and then present a compelling opportunity

(invitation) to the lucky prospect framed in terms that plug into the prospect's own motivation strategy.

Motivation is the key first step. Some folks have what they call a "fear of selling." Others have various shades of reticence to "selling" because they're "too busy," or give one of a number of "good" reasons from their point of view for not taking biz dev actions. This inaction needs to be superseded by sufficient motivation.

Motivation can be: money, fame, recognition, promotion, performance targets, the new house, 24-hour care givers for a parent, etc. Ask each member of the law firm, "What's important to you?" See the book's Index for more on, "What's important to you?" It takes a skilled coach using body, voice and eye access cues to know when true motivation is being elicited.

Technique is teachable. The firm must provide business development training from a skilled trainer-coach. Train every member of the law firm in basic sales and rapport skills. Train and test. Train and test.

The biz dev coach must verify that the firm member possesses the two essential "must haves" for a person to actively develop new business, motivation and technique.

Check motivation. What's important to the firm member about their law practice? Then what's important to them about bringing in new business?

Eliminate the fear of selling. If you have an honest-to-gosh fear or phobia of selling, a Master in NLP, neurolinguistic programming, should be able to dramatically reduce or eliminate that issue. If you don't have anyone trained in addressing phobias, contact this author for assistance.

In the neurolinguistic programming, NLP, process, the scary "fear" that blocks motivation and action can usually be "overpowered" by a newly anchored internal interpretation that minimizes the stopping action of the old fear. Then, a compelling motivator is added and anchored. A Master NLP biz dev coach will work with the firm member to find a sufficiently powerful motivator and "load" that up with a positive anchor (a neurosynaptic trigger selected by the party receiving the coaching.)

Technique has a number of bite-sized facets. One part of a successful new business technique is to use a Business Development Action Sheet.

It's helpful to identify and list a "key metric" that can be easily tracked on the Business Development Action Sheet. A key metric comes out of a ratio that is generally involved in generating new business.

An example of a key metric would be, "we've noticed, on average, it takes about 9 calls, two meetings and a formal written proposal before a prospect is ready to review a contract for services." This information gives us three metrics to work on each month: number of calls, number of meetings and number of written proposals.

Another metric comes out of the verbal offer-to-acceptance ratio.

Before one pre-qualified prospect says, "yes", how many total prospects, on average, need to hear this simple offer, "Would you like our firm to help you achieve your goals?"

How many categories of responses are there to the question, "Would you like our firm to help you achieve your goals?" Basically, there are four: yes, a qualified yes, a qualified no, and no. All of these answers can lead to a contract for services. You just need to know the "technique."

Maybe the firm's experience is that, on average, you need to make six offers to get to an unqualified "yes." So, in that simplified example, in order to achieve one new business matter agreement per month, you're goal would be to put yourself in at least six situations a month where you can make the offer, "Would you like our firm to help you achieve your goals?"

A Business Development Action Sheet is a very helpful tool that can address both motivation and technique.

Use one Business Development Action Sheet to help the lawyer and his coach to identify and track the big picture annual goals.

Use a different Business Development Action Sheet to list those individual weekly, or monthly, action steps that will support achieving the annual goals. This is the "chunk-it-down" action sheet. This is the sheet which includes the key metrics being tracked along with all the other essential specifics, like the actual names of the prospects being approached, the intra-firm education meetings to be held, the targeted client discussions regarding possible new matters, lectures, conferences, networking events, billable hours, etc.

It can be very helpful if the lawyer knows that conversations with the business development coach are confidential allowing for clearly defined exceptions where certain issues and results go to the CMO and Managing Partner.

Two Business Development Action Sheet examples follow.

Business Development Action Sheet : Annual

Billing year 20____ $____ /Year $____ /Qtr $____ /Mo

Standard Rate:____ Realization Rate:____ New Client Origination:____ New Matter Origination:____

Annual Working attorney Collections: $____,000 Annual Billing Attorney Collections: $____,000

	Prospect/ Client/Other	Desired Outcome/ Goal/Advancement	By When	Next Step(s)
1				
2				
3				
4				
5				
6				
7				
8				
9				
10				
11				
12				
13				
14				
15				

Business Development Action Sheet: Weekly Plan vs Actual — 101WaysToGrowAThrivingLawPractice.com

	Plan: Specific Actions Client 1 Prospect Meetings, Matters, Metrics, Biz Dev Meetings, Conferences, Train, Lecture, Article, Calls, Verbal Offer, Proposal, CLE, etc. Qtr _____ / 20 ___ Month of _____ / 20 ___ Week of ___ / ___ / 20 ___	Actual: D: Done N: Not Done P: Partial	Notes:
1			
2			
3			
4			
5			
6			
7			
8			
9			
10			
11			
12			
13			
14			
15			

Expanded Business Development Quiz

To rate the firm's business development, eight broad categories have been created below to facilitate thinking and talking about various aspects of building the practice.

Now rate current accomplishment level of each numbered specific Business Development Activity: 0 to 10 points.

You decide how many points to give the firm. Each numbered item can be given a max of 10 plus 5 bonus points, if media has acknowledged the firm as an expert in a given area. Sub sets of a numbered item should be given a portion of 10 points.

Every business will grade each item with a slightly different slant. That's OK. Just try to be consistent.

Don't sweat over a few points on an item either way.

This is an internal score, and one you can share with your Business Development Consultant / Coach and your Marketing Director.

Each item should be treated as having a maximum score of 10 points with 5 bonus points (15 total) if firm is recognized by the media as the best (or expert) in the geo area the firm serves.

Examples:

        10 = Maximum research in identified research area
        10 = Maximum result / achievement in geo area
served
        15 = Bonus: If press / media have recognized the firm
as   expert in identified area

In the first section, Research, give the firm 10 points for an item if maximum research has been done in the area identified.

Following point levels are only guides for a national firm.
If the firm is best in its geo-area that's a10.

Business Development Activities Rating Table

Category: Business Development Professionals

Item #	Business Development Professionals Quiz questions #1 to #3 for this business area are in the front section of the book.	Rate Level 0 to 10 Points
4	Is the firm aware of the personality research on how to make good lawyers into new business rainmakers? Notes / Comments / Action Items:	
5	Does firm have a Business Development consultant full time, part-time, occasionally, or no one yet? Notes / Comments / Action Items:	
6	Does firm have a marketing consultant full time, part-time, occasionally or no one yet? Notes / Comments / Action Items:	
7	Does firm have a publicist, or public relations specialist: full-time, part-time, occasionally, or no one yet? Notes / Comments / Action Items:	

8	Does firm use an advertising company full time, part-time, occasionally, or no one yet? Notes / Comments / Action Items:	
9	Does firm have a list of freelance writers and uses them full time, part-time, occasionally, or no one yet? Notes / Comments / Action Items:	
10	Does firm have a list of all legal field contacts at all major media, e.g. local, national, magazine, newspaper, radio, TV, e-letters, professional organizations, etc. whose core audience overlaps with the firm's target audience? Notes / Comments / Action Items:	
11	Has firm interviewed (if only for business development ideas, and to have as a stand-by resource) a law firm business development company, e.g. Keller Business Development Group? www.KellerBusinessDevelopmentGroup.com Notes / Comments / Action Items:	

12	Has firm asked for return-on-investment (ROI) analysis of dollars invested in business development consulting, coaching and training? Notes / Comments / Action Items:	
13	Does firm have a professional law practice business development consultant? If "no", have you read the California Lawyer magazine article on same? Has firm gotten a free meeting and free proposal from a professional law practice business development consultant-coach-trainer? Notes / Comments / Action Items:	
14	Does firm have a professional law practice business development consultant? If "no", have you read the California Lawyer magazine article on same? Has firm gotten a free meeting and free proposal from a professional law practice business development consultant-coach-trainer? Notes / Comments / Action Items:	

Category: **Essential Basic Research**

Item #	**Research** Quiz questions #1 to #21 for this business area are in the front section of the book.	**Rate Level** 0 to 10 Points
22	Clients. Most clients have come from which practice area(s)? Notes / Comments / Action Items:	
23	Who? Who needs the firm's services within each practice area? Notes / Comments / Action Items:	
24	Geo. Where geographically are the identified people and businesses who need the firm's services? Notes / Comments / Action Items:	
25	Rain. How many rainmakers are in the firm? Notes / Comments / Action Items:	

26	Rain. How many law practice rainmakers do you know that will consult with the firm? Notes / Comments / Action Items:	
27	Prospects. Has the firm made a list of the competitions' client list, labeled as Column "A", and asked why they aren't the firm's clients? Has the firm made a list of all companies competing with each of those clients in Column "A", labeled Column "B"? Is firm using Column "B" as a prospect list? (Is firm keeping track of Column "A" as an on-going prospect list?) Notes / Comments / Action Items:	
28	Cash. Has the firm answered the question, "where is the money in my business?" Notes / Comments / Action Items:	
29	Rep. What is the firm's reputation? With the media? With our target audience(s)? Notes / Comments / Action Items:	

30	Competition. What are competitors doing to generate clients? Notes / Comments / Action Items:	
31	Revenue. Does the firm know how firm has gotten past clients? Notes / Comments / Action Items:	
32	Growth. Has the firm looked at the potential benefit of merging firms / divisions? Notes / Comments / Action Items:	
33	Subs. Does the firm have a list of sub-contractors accessible to support various practices as needed? Notes / Comments / Action Items:	
34	Associations. Has firm approached largest associations for part-time counsel such as condos, yacht clubs, homeowner associations, etc. for a fee, or free exposure to select groups? Notes / Comments / Action Items:	

35	Endeca. Has firm researched Endeca? Notes / Comments / Action Items:	
36	Ask. Does firm have a policy of regularly asking people in the business community how would they promote the firm's business? Notes / Comments / Action Items:	
37	Media. Has the firm interviewed at least 4 media, video, and TV documentary production companies for promo video ideas, e.g. a video for YouTube.com, press video clips, etc.? Notes / Comments / Action Items:	
38	TV. Has the firm interviewed at least 4 local / regional / Statewide / national TV stations' advertising and media-buy sales managers for their promotional ideas? Notes / Comments / Action Items:	

39	Radio. Has the firm interviewed at least 4 local / regional / Statewide / national radio stations' advertising and media-buy sales managers for ideas? Notes / Comments / Action Items:	
40	News. Has the firm interviewed the local newspapers' advertising and media-buy sales managers for their promotional ideas? Notes / Comments / Action Items:	
41	National. Has the firm interviewed the national newspapers' advertising and media-buy sales managers for their promotional ideas? Notes / Comments / Action Items:	
42	Press. Has the firm interviewed the local, regional, State, and national legal publications' advertising and media-buy sales managers for their promotional ideas? Notes / Comments / Action Items:	

43	Newsletters. Has the firm interviewed the local advertising and media-buy sales managers for all local organizations' newsletters and magazines for their promotional ideas? Notes / Comments / Action Items:	
44	Publications. Has the firm asked every member of the firm to submit all alumni, sorority and fraternity publication media contacts for stories, articles, news announcements, and possible ad space buys? Notes / Comments / Action Items:	
45	Affiliates. Does the firm have affiliate offices in every major City, either formal or informal, that the firm can contact on a moment's notice? Notes / Comments / Action Items:	
46	Competitors. Has the firm put together a professional study and report on the top 10 competitors' business development techniques including advertising, marketing, media buys, etc.? (Hint: as the firm interviews each of the	

46 cont.	advertising, marketing, media, public relations, free lance writers and event planning firms, ask them what other law firms have they done work for, and ask them to show samples of the work they have done for these other firms.) Notes / Comments / Actions Items:	
47	Culture. Has the firm identified non-English speaking interpreters for every major culture in the firm's market area? Notes / Comments / Action Items:	
48	Cross-culture. Has the firm then asked every non-English speaking interpreter in its market area to keep the firm in mind, as you will keep them in mind, for future business opportunities? Notes / Comments / Action Items:	
49	SEO. Has the firm interviewed a number of SEO, Search Engine Optimization, consultants? What did the firm learn from each interview? Has the firm taken action to raise its SEO rating? Notes / Comments / Action Items:	

50	Who's Who? Has the firm listed the "leading attorneys" in the community? In each practice area? Has the firm listed the actions that made them the "leading" attorneys in their area? Notes / Comments / Action Items:	
51	Rep. What is the reputation of each attorney in the firm? Can one or more of these reputations be leveraged even more? Notes / Comments / Action Items:	
52	Does the firm know what legal work potential clients (individuals, government agencies, businesses, and other organizations need that the firm does not offer? Does the firm have a relationship with an attorney or firm in each of those areas? Is it quid pro quo? Notes / Comments / Action Items:	
53	Affiliates. Has the firm reviewed all law firms in the firm's market area and asked, "What services does the firm offer that they don't?" And has the firm then outreached to those firms to offer the firm's services on an as needed basis (thus expanding the services the other firms can offer their clientele)? A classic win-win. Notes / Comments / Action Items:	

54	Expand. Has the firm reviewed what outside resources the firm can hire, or have on call, to facilitate the firm's growth and expansion? Notes / Comments / Action Items:	
55	Languages. How many total languages do members of the firm speak? Notes / Comments / Action Items:	
56	Cross-sell. Does the firm very carefully, skillfully, and with great diplomacy cross-sell with the firm's existing client base? (For clients that are bosom buddies, you simply jokingly ask them every month how are they doing on their marketing quota of at least one new referral a month? Or ask, "What other departments or divisions within your company could use our firm's awesome legal skills?") Notes / Comments / Action Items:	
57	Stretch. Is the firm exploring expanding into new markets? Notes / Comments / Action Items:	

58	Alertness. Is every member of the firm comfortably on alert for low cost, high profile ways to put the firm's name in front of a large number of people? With examples periodically emailed to all firm personnel? Notes / Comments / Action Items:	
59	Goals. When running a business development goal-setting meeting, does the firm have at least one person present who is trained in the proper definition and formatting structure for creating a "well formed desired outcome"? (See www.100WaysToG rowAThrivingLawPractice.com for a definition and proper structure.) Notes / Comments / Action Items:	
60	Counsel. Has the firm developed a list of the top 500 small to medium businesses and assigned someone to call them to offer the firm's services as outside counsel? Notes / Comments / Action Items:	
61	Largest. Does the firm know who the 500 largest companies are in the firm's market area, and whether or not they have in-house counsel? Notes / Comments / Action Items:	

62	Lunch. Has the firm taken retired successful lawyers to lunch and inquired if they have any ideas that might assist the firm's business development growth? Notes / Comments / Action Items:	
63	Conferences. Is the firm attending the trade conferences that the firm's clients and prospective clients are attending? Notes / Comments / Action Items:	
64	CPA. Does the firm have a strong working relationship with every major CPA and accounting firm in the area as a resource for their services, and as resource for business referrals? Notes / Comments / Action Items:	

Category: Internet

Item #	**Internet** Quiz questions #1 to #8 for this business area are in the front section of the book.	Rate Level 0 to 10 Points
9	Does the firm (or any of the attorneys) have a blog? Notes / Comments / Action Items:	
10	Does the firm have a website (1pt)? Does the firm have a full-time (8pts) or part-time (6), or on-call (3) website manager? Is some news, firm calendar, or other element of the website updated daily (8pts), weekly (6), monthly (4), quarterly (2), or rarely? Has the firm listed every possible practice area offered by the firm on the firm's web-site? Notes / Comments / Action Items:	
11	Is each attorney registered on Facebook (with access by formal approval only)?* (There is a reason a Chinese investor paid $100 million for 2% of Facebook.) *= worth repeating. Notes / Comments / Action Items:	

12	Is each attorney registered on Twitter? Notes / Comments / Action Items:	
13	Does firm have at least one legal lecture video on YouTube, Flicker, Doggs, MySpace, Plaxo, Wikipedia, or other video website? Notes / Comments / Action Items:	
14	What is the firm's SEO, Search Engine Optimization, rating? (This was mentioned in Research because it is so important to business development.) When I Google or Bing the firm's name, how high on the list does the firm's name appear? How many listings? Notes / Comments / Action Items:	
15	What is the SEO of each member of the firm by name? Notes / Comments / Action Items:	

16	Are there resources on firm's website that drive clients and not-yet-clients to site? Latest examples of these magnets are in the book, or go to www.100WaysToGrow AThrivingLawPractice.com articles _ SEO. Notes / Comments / Action Items:	
17	What is the SEO of each member of the firm by individual name? Notes / Comments / Action Items:	
18	Is any of the firm's search engine info found on Google or Bing negative? Does the firm need to flood Google and Bing with positive news to force the negative news on to pages way beyond page one of the search engine report? Does the firm know how to achieve best SEO? (See SEO strategy on www. 100WaysToGrowAThrivingLawPractice.com). Notes / Comments / Action Items:	

◇◇

Category: Network

Item #	**Network** Quiz questions #1 to #13 for this business area are in the front section of the book.	Rate Level 0 - 10 Points
14	How many U.S. Senators and U.S. Congressional Reps have firm members advising them? Which ones? Notes / Comments / Action Items:	
15	How many "Attorneys-for-(political office candidate)" committees have firm members (been) involved? Which ones? Notes / Comments / Action Items:	
16	Community. How many schools, churches or other community groups have a firm member on their boards or key committees? Notes / Comments / Action Items:	
17	Culture. How many multi-cultural organizations have a firm member as member? Which ones? How many? Any board or key committee position? Notes / Comments / Action Items:	

18	Has everyone, everyone, everyone been asked for business leads? Notes / Comments / Action Items:	
19	The President of the United States. How many firm members are involved with U.S Presidential politics, committees? Notes / Comments / Action Items:	
20	Republican and Democratic National politics. How many firm members are involved with a national political party on a national, State, or County level? Notes / Comments / Action Items:	
21	Is the firm known within its community? Do you have 3 or more ideas on how to improve and expand your reputation? Notes / Comments / Action Items:	
22	Philosophical leaders. Have members of the firm sought networking support from their respective spiritual leaders, priests, rabbis, and ministers? Notes / Comments / Action Items:	

23	Politicians. How many retired politicians have you and other firm members taken to lunch, or breakfast, in the last 6 months? Notes / Comments / Action Items:	
24	Professors. How many law professors have firm members taken to lunch? Notes / Comments / Action Items:	
25	Women. How many women in your firm can teach (mentor) other women the art of high level business networking? Notes / Comments / Action Items:	
26	Gym. Am I and other firm members dropping simple little remarks at the health club about what we do to the other regulars we run into day in and day out? Notes / Comments / Action Items:	

27	AG. How close is the firm to the State and U.S. Attorney General? Notes / Comments / Action Items:	
28	DA. How close is the firm to the State and local district attorney? Notes / Comments / Action Items:	
29	Relatives. Has the firm explored the fruit of its members' family trees? Notes / Comments / Action Items:	
30	Parents. How many firm members' parents have friends who would derive great pleasure in assisting their friend's "kids?" Notes / Comments / Action Items:	
31	Business Contacts. Utilizing Business Connections to Grow Business. Are firm members telling everyone they give money to (bankers, insurance agents, accountants, plastic surgeons, architects, plumbers, senior trades people, Fed-Ex, UPS, etc.) that they would like to "cross-promote" each other's business? Have they taken the largest of these to lunch or coffee? Notes / Comments / Action Items:	

32	Does the firm know its local and County library directors by their first name? More importantly, do these know the firm? Are these very well connected people on your holiday card mailing list? Notes / Comments / Action Items:	
33	Have you considered a "trade" or barter with an essential business supplier? Notes / Comments / Action Items:	
34	Lawyers. When was the last time a firm member took a retired successful lawyer to lunch? Notes / Comments / Action Items:	
35	Chambers. How many Chambers of Commerce count you and other firm members as members? Notes / Comments / Action Items:	
36	Socialize. How many monthly events do firm members attend which are also attended by clients and prospects? Notes / Comments / Action Items:	

37	Sports. Which sports do members enjoy along with other high achievers? Notes / Comments / Action Items:	
38	Civil. Are firm members keenly aware that civil servants at every level meet people who need lawyers? Notes / Comments / Action Items:	
39	Bridges. Are you always inviting firm members to build new bridges to people who may be conduits to new business? Notes / Comments / Action Items:	
40	How many judicial advisory and legislative advisory committees have firm's members on them? Which ones? Notes / Comments / Action Items:	

Category: Marketing

This next section includes advertising, public relations, press and media relations. This section includes key actions that cause someone to think of the firm and feel positively about the firm. It goes without saying that Marketing, Advertising, Public Relations, Press and Media relations are distinct disciplines with trained specialists required for proper focus within that given discipline, e.g. the firm's Legal Marketing expert.

Ultimately, all of these outreach activities are designed to reinforce a current client's decision to stay with the firm and to cause prospective new clients to contact the firm as a result of a positive message, thought, or experience involving the firm.

Item #	**Marketing** Quiz questions #1 to #16 for this business area are in the front section of the book.	Rate Level 0 to 10 Points
17	Is it your policy to periodically send a congratu-latory (or thank you) card and/or gift or note to someone you read about in the news (good deed acknowledgement)? Notes / Comments / Action Items:	

18	Has the business sponsored any thing of benefit to the community in the past year? Ever? Notes / Comments / Action Items:	
19	Have you considered sponsoring a modest scholarship at the local school, college, university, or law school. Notes / Comments / Action Items:	
20	E-zines and emails. Does firm have a daily, weekly, or monthly email that goes out to an ever increasing mailing list? (305 c) Notes / Comments / Action Items:	
21	Charities. Auction. Has firm donated a free hour of legal consulting as part of a charity's auction or silent auction? Notes / Comments / Action Items:	
22	Public office. Has anyone in the firm run for an elected office? Notes / Comments / Action Items:	

23	Community involvement. Any firm member coach a Little League team? Notes / Comments / Action Items:	
24	Get 'em to beat a path to your front door. Has firm done the math on opening its lobby to a charitable event? Notes / Comments / Action Items:	
25	Free. Pavlov + 5th Ave marketing. When someone does come to the firm, does the firm give them something FREE to take home that has your website and phone number on it in addition to a business card? Notes / Comments / Action Items:	
26	Does the firm regularly issue press releases? Notes / Comments / Action Items:	
27	Do you or other firm members teach a course, or periodically give lectures that can help grow the business? Notes / Comments / Action Items:	

28	Is a firm member an officer of legal association? Notes / Comments / Action Items:	
29	Is the firm advertising in some medium? Notes / Comments / Action Items:	
30	Has the firm considered a tasteful bumper sticker like Smart & Brilliant Supports Children's Hospital? Notes / Comments / Action Items:	
31	Does the practice have a unique legal specialty not offered by many firms in the market area? Do all the other firms that could use this specialty know this? Notes / Comments / Action Items:	
32	Culture. Does the firm actively teach all members, with examples, that anyone and everyone can be a finder or source of legal business? Notes / Comments / Action Items:	
33	Website. Has the firm created ten to one hundred reasons for non-clients to come to firm's website? Notes / Comments / Action Items:	

34	How many firm ads are out there? Where? Total ad audience? Target audience(s) identified? Notes / Comments / Action Items:	
35	Do firm's ads, website, and promotional material all have key marketing buzz words? Notes / Comments / Action Items:	
36	Does the firm or any firm member have a blog? Notes / Comments / Action Items:	
37	Are there blogs that members of firm contribute to? Notes / Comments / Action Items:	
38	Google. How high on a search does the firm come up when various practice areas in your market geo area are Googled and Binged? Do you note who comes up ahead of you and ask yourself, "Why"? Notes / Comments / Action Items:	

39	Like the White House, CNN, 311 and cities like San Francisco, does the firm participate in Twitter? Notes / Comments / Action Items:	
40	Press. How many press and media contacts does the firm have? How many for each different media outlet: magazines, newspaper, radio, e-zines and TV? Notes / Comments / Action Items:	
41	Media. Are you aware of the blogs run by the media in your town? Does the firm ever contribute to those blogs? Notes / Comments / Action Items:	
42	Public speaking. How many public speaking engagements will firm participate in this year? Notes / Comments / Action Items:	
43	Media. On Memorial Day does firm honor veterans with an ad in the local paper? Does firm have one or more veterans who can speak at a Memorial Day event? Notes / Comments / Action Items:	

44	Website. Does firm's website offer useful articles and links in various areas of general interest to clients and prospects? Notes / Comments / Action Items:	
45	Website. Does firm's website offer links to all key elected political offices? (251, 253) Notes / Comments / Action Items:	
46	Website. Does firm's website offer links to all key local, County, State and Federal government services? (251, 254, 255) Notes / Comments / Action Items:	
47	CLE. Are firm members giving or taking CLE courses? Notes / Comments / Action Items:	
48	Reciprocity. How many businesses or services does your firm promote that can refer business to you? Notes / Comments / Action Items:	

49	How many free public talks will members of the firm present this year? Notes / Comments / Action Items:	
50	Has any firm member run for public office? Notes / Comments / Action Items:	
51	Any firm member a featured speaker at a trade conference? Notes / Comments / Action Items:	
52	Has any firm member published a legal book? Notes / Comments / Action Items:	
53	Does the firm have a "press release potential" mentality? Notes / Comments / Action Items:	
54	Are all key media outlets aware of your firm as a possible source for comment on certain subjects? Notes / Comments / Action Items:	

55	Does the firm ever speak at a peer event? Notes / Comments / Action Items:	
56	Direct mail. Have you investigated a targeted direct mail using the free research of at least 3 direct mail services? Notes / Comments / Action Items:	
57	Are you a member of LMA, Legal Marketing Association? Notes / Comments / Action Items:	
58	Does the firm have a trademarked logo? Notes / Comments / Action Items:	
59	How many legal bar association committees have your firm as a member? Notes / Comments / Action Items:	
60	How many court advisory panels have your firm as a member? Notes / Comments / Action Items:	

61	How many local / national non-profit organizations have your firm as a member? Notes / Comments / Action Items:	
62	Does the firm have a provision for "Pre-Paid Legal"? Notes / Comments / Action Items:	
63	Are there any noteworthy memberships listed on the firm's website? How many? Notes / Comments / Action Items:	
64	Free. Free 24 hr publicity. Has the firm given away something with firm's name on it in a charity event, e.g. a t-shirt at a local charity run? Notes / Comments / Action Items:	
65	Sponsor. Event. Speaker. Has firm sponsored a unique event or celebrated speaker? Notes / Comments / Action Items:	

66	Press op. Has firm gone green and issued a press release about same? Notes / Comments / Action Items:	
67	Media. How often does firm take a legal writer, editor, publisher to lunch? Notes / Comments / Action Items:	
68	Politics. Has firm interviewed various political campaign directors for their business contacts and "awareness campaign" strategies? Notes / Comments / Action Items:	
69	Public Service Resource. How many government and public service resources can be found on my website? Notes / Comments / Action Items:	
70	Write. What have I, or members of the firm, gotten published in last 24 months? Notes / Comments / Action Items:	

71	Expert. In what areas is the firm considered "expert" within geo area, by local media? Notes / Comments / Action Items:	
72	Publish. In what journals or news media have firm members been positively quoted? (174) Notes / Comments / Action Items:	
73	Path. How many ways is the firm getting people to beat a path to its door, literally, before they (or their referrals) need us? Notes / Comments / Action Items:	
74	Press. What's getting press and am I always asking how the firm can positively associate with something securing public attention? Notes / Comments / Action Items:	
75	Media. Does the firm have media consciousness? Are members of the firm regularly asking, "What are we doing, or could be doing, that would qualify for a press release?" Notes / Comments / Action Items:	

76	Solver. Is the firm known as a problem solver, a "can do", firm? Notes / Comments / Action Items:	
77	Play. Are you and firm members socializing a la Warren Buffett? Notes / Comments / Action Items:	
78	Links. Does firm offer web links on its website to firm-approved charities? Notes / Comments / Action Items:	
79	Politics. Has firm interviewed the guy / gal who came in 2nd in a political campaign for their "awareness campaign" strategies, promo ideas, and community contacts (group, individual, media) and what specific advice would they give you to get your firm "elected" by potential clients? Notes / Comments / Action Items:	

80	Has firm done a video worthy of You-Tube.com? Notes / Comments / Action Items:	
81	Is every firm member verifiably versed in an optimal 30 second sound bite describing the business? Does the sound bite describe specialties while making it clear that the firm has available resources allowing for new clients? Has firm distributed to its members examples of a 5 second, 15 second, 30 second, 60 second and 2 minute firm promo sound bite? Notes / Comments / Action Items:	

◇◇◇

Category: Goodwill

Item #	**Goodwill** Quiz questions #1 to #3 for this business area are in the front section of the book.	Rate Level 0 to 10 Points
4	Goodwill. Has the firm done something for the public good like the White House did in creating a public garden? Notes / Comments / Action Items:	

5	Goodwill. Charity. Community. Has firm been a sponsor of a charitable event, or popular community event? Or sponsored a charity's website? Notes / Comments / Action Items:	
6	Goodwill. Has firm paid for the printing of a community charitable event handout with firm's name mentioned on the form? Notes / Comments / Action Items:	
7	Goodwill. Happy Birthday! How many birthday cards does your firm send out annually? Notes / Comments / Action Items:	
8	Goodwill. Is someone in your firm mentoring the local law school fraternity / sorority? Notes / Comments / Action Items:	
9	Free. Goodwill and PR. 24 hour advertising. Does the firm give away something free to everyone who comes to the firm's office that has a utility value? Does the firm give away something free outside the office with firm's name on it at a fund raiser of some sort? Notes / Comments / Action Items:	

10	Goodwill. Does the firm actively support its local, City, County, and State law enforcement agencies? Notes / Comments / Action Items:	
11	Goodwill. Has firm done something lately to help someone: the elderly, the infirmed, the homeless, anyone? Notes / Comments / Action Items:	
12	Donate. Has firm fixed a community service room or building? Notes / Comments / Action Items:	
13	Volunteerism. Does firm have a culture of supporting community volunteer work? Notes / Comments / Action Items:	
14	Goodwill. Has firm taken on any cases pro bono that will generate community (client and prospective client) goodwill? Notes / Comments / Action Items:	

15	Goodwill. Heart. Has firm built goodwill fast by placing carefully selected firm-approved 501C3 links on firm's website? Notes / Comments / Action Items:	

◇◇◇◇◇◇◇◇◇◇◇◇◇◇◇◇◇◇◇◇◇◇◇◇◇◇◇◇◇◇◇◇◇◇◇◇◇◇◇

Category: Administration

Administration includes the classic operational activities as well as oversight of every essential element of maintaining and growing the firm's business. Senior management is ultimately responsible for growing the law practice. Management through its administrative procedures must instill a business development mentality within every aspect of the firm's operations, from answering phones to sending out invoices.

Item #	**Administration** Quiz questions #1 to #4 for this business area are in front of book.	Rate Level 0 to 10 Points
5	How many in the firm look at the business development plan, or their portion of it, daily? Weekly? Monthly? Notes / Comments / Action Items:	

6	Does every member of firm have a business development plan? Do they look at it weekly? Notes / Comments / Action Items:	
7	Does every member of the firm have a business development coach they can call confidentially at any time? Notes / Comments / Action Items: :	
8	Money. Where is it? Has management identified the top ten revenue sources in its fields of practice? Notes / Comments / Action Items:	
9	Has management asked each member of the firm to submit at least 10 marketing ideas to the Chief Marketing Officer or General Manager? Notes / Comments / Action Items:	
10	Does management have a list of at least 500 companies, people, groups that could hire the firm? Notes / Comments / Action Items:	

11	Does firm have a full time marketing director or part-time business development consultant who also provides firm-wide training as well as one-on-one business development coaching to individual attorneys, as needed? Notes / Comments / Action Items:	
12	Holydays. Is the firm and each individual attorney sensitive to various cultural and religious holidays and holydays? Notes / Comments / Action Items:	
13	List. Does the firm have a business development list? Is the firm doing the list? Notes / Comments / Action Items:	

◇◇

Category: Image

Item #	**Image** External: Reputation; Internal: Culture Quiz questions #1 to #4 for this business area are in the front section of the book.	Rate Level: 0 - 10 Points
5	Health. Am I and other firm members as healthy as can be? Am I setting a good example for all other members of the firm? Notes / Comments / Action Items:	

6	Balance. Are members of firm demonstrating healthy balance whenever possible? Notes / Comments / Action Items:	
7	Responsive. Is your rep that you return all calls same day? Emails? Same thing? Notes / Comments / Action Items:	
8	Does firm have a culture of always looking for and congratulating a job well done? Notes / Comments / Action Items:	
9	Firm Culture. Does firm have a "can do" culture? Notes / Comments / Action Items:	
10	Does firm inculcate "everyone, everyone, everyone is a possible source of business, or business referral"? Does firm send out the occasional memo reminding everyone in the firm that their next conversation with the mail person or hairdresser could just bring in "the next big one"? Notes / Comments / Action Items:	

◇◇

Category: Legal World Presence

Item #	**Legal World Presence** Quiz questions #1 to #7 for this business area are in front of book.	Rate Level 0 to 10 Points
8	Does firm belong to National, State, County, City ABA? Notes / Comments / Action Items:	
9	Are any firm attorneys referenced in a precedent-setting case? Notes / Comments / Action Items:	
10	Does firm have good press / media contacts in radio and TV as well as national, State, regional, county, local legal publications? Notes / Comments / Action Items:	

11	Does firm have a Professor for Legal CLE courses? Notes / Comments / Action Items:	
12	How many firm members have authored legal articles? Notes / Comments / Action Items:	
13	Is firm a member of specialty bar associations like Elder Law, etc? Notes / Comments / Action Items:	
14	How many other law firms, larger or smaller, is firm affiliated with either formally or informally? Notes / Comments / Action Items:	

15	How many different media know firm as a resource? Notes / Comments / Action Items:	
16	How many legal books have firm members authored? Notes / Comments / Action Items:	
17	Firm Culture. Does firm have a culture of always looking for and congratulating a job well done? Notes / Comments / Action Items:	
18	Firm Culture. Does firm have a "can do" culture? Notes / Comments / Action Items:	

19	Does firm inculcate that "everyone, everyone, everyone is a possible source of business, or business referral"? Does firm send out the occasional memo reminding everyone in the firm that their next conversation with the mail person or hairdresser could just bring in "the next big one"? Notes / Comments / Action Items:	

List of all the Ways referenced herein.

27.4   Network: Tap into your family's network.

27.5   Network: Where do you frequent?

27.6   Network: Go to alumni meetings. Hand out 10 cards.

27.7   Network: Remember, everyone is a source for new business.

27.8   Network: Grow your business the old fashioned way.

27.9   Network: Talk to everyone.

27.1   Network: Ask your clients for business referrals.

28.1   Eat to win: Have a six figure lunch.

28.2   Eat to win: Take a retired successful lawyer to lunch.

28.2   Eat to win: Take legal professors to lunch -- from your
        law school and from other law schools.

28.3   Eat to win: Take a retired politician to lunch.

29.1   Work the VAKOG: Always, always have something sweet and
        FREE in your reception area.

29.2   Work the VAKOG: FREE lattes.

29.3   Work the VAKOG: Chocolate.

30.1   FREE. Give something of value for FREE.

30.2   FREE: Give a FREE gift that keeps on selling you.

30.3   FREE: GreenFree. Give the eco gift that keeps giving.

30.4   FRE: FREE to you. FREE to your client.

30.5   FREE: Secure ongoing FREE advertising by going into the clothing
        business.

30.6   FREE: Give away something free.

31   Hire a marketing employee and receive many FREE promo ideas during
        the interview process.

32   Borrow good ideas.

33   Interview political campaign managers.

34   Make "seconds" your new first.

35   Interview 5 freelance press release writers.

36.1   Survey: Bite the bullet and do a client satisfaction survey.

36.2   Survey: Conduct a client satisfaction survey: Part 2.

37.1   Enhance or change your reputation.

37.2   Enhance or change your reputation: Purchase a few well-placed ads,
        articles, event sponsorships, and charity fundraisers.

38   Don't let your fingers do the walking.

39.1   Get people beating a trail to your door.

39.2   Get people beating a trail to your door: Part Two.

40   Let art attract new clients.

41.1   Think Triple R: Invite folks to the Triple R ranch.

41.2   Think Triple R: reciprocal referral relationships.

41.3   Think Triple R: Contact every major CPA firm in your area.

41.4 Think Triple R: Contact a local hotel business owner.

42 Find cross-promote relationships.

43 Hire the top marketing director from a competitive firm.

44.1 No harm in asking: Ask everyone you speak with, "If you were in charge of growing my business, what would you do?"

44.2 No harm in asking: Bond with people who hire attorneys.

44.2 No harm in asking: Bond with people who know people who hire attorneys.

45.1 Think Press: Become the "go-to expert" quoted by the media.

45.2 Think Press: Create an on-camera video of you being interviewed on your subject of expertise.

45.3 Think Press: Issue a press release.

45.4 Think Press: Seize opportunities to secure press by doing good.

45.5 Think Press: Become the "expert" in your field.

46.1 Press on: Cultivate relationships with the press.

46.2 Press on: Do something that merits an award.

46.3 Press on: Insert yourself into the news.

46.4 Press on: Save the planet.

47.1 Network like a pro: Join LinkedIn.com.

47.2 Network like a pro: Join FaceBook.

47.3 Network like a pro: Tweet, if you can.

47.4 Network like a pro: BLOG

48 Flex your E-Power with an e-zine.

49 Become the out-sourced legal arm of small to medium sized businesses.

50 Do something worthy of a YouTube.com video in your area of expertise.

51.1 Business Card Combo: Try the David King Keller business card + gift card combo idea.

51.2 Business Card Combo: Try the David King Keller business card + gift card combo idea. Part Two.

51.3 Business Card Combo: Give away something FREE when you hand out your contact information.

52 Make informal interview calls to a list of sub-contractor attorneys.

53.1 Affiliate: Do business with other law firms.

53.2 Affiliate: Merge firms.

53.3 Affiliate: Contact law firms in your area that do not offer your particular service.

53.4 Affiliate: What you can't do can help you.

54.1 Advertise! Who? Where?

54.2 Advertise! Improve on what the competition is doing.

55 Go green.

56.1 Sponsor a benefit lunch: in honor of a retired or retiring judge.

56.2   Sponsor a benefit lunch: in honor of a retired or retiring politician.
56.3   Sponsor a benefit lunch: for a local or national icon.
57   Contact the 50 largest condo boards and Home Owners' Associations (HOAs) in your area.
58   Have a pop-chocolate quiz.
59   Offer to sponsor the printing of an event's brochure.
60   Donate legal time to a charitable auction.
61   Coach a Little League team.
62.1   Connect: with the well connected.
62.2   Connect: Be social.
62.3   Connect: Go where the business people go to meet.
62.4   Connect: Each firm member should be involved with at least one local charity.
62.5   Connect: Take up a sport that forms relationships.
63.1   Join: a community organization. Where? Who?
63.2   Join: a few impressive organizations.
63.3   Join: a club frequented by prospective clients.
64.1   Lead and connect: Become a Board member.
64.2   Lead and connect: Join a community organization.
65.1   Join a legal org: e.g. become an officer of your local legal association.
65.2   Join a legal org: e.g. become a committee member the national bar association.
65.3   Join a legal org: e.g. become a committee member of a State or County court advisory and rule making commission.
66.1   Go to Chamber of Commerce business-to-business mixers.
66.2   Go to Chamber of Commerce business-to-business mixers.
67   Know thyself.
68   Win with humor.
69.1   Relax: Have more fun.
69.2   Relax: Write, read, pray, meditate . . .
70   Don't buy into any advice about limits.
71   Write a book on your subject.
72   Get free on-line time management suggestions / support.
73.1   Speak: Get their attention when you speak.
73.2   Speak: to your community.
73.3   Speak: Make two to four public speaking engagements a year.
73.4   Speak: Give a free talk.
73.5   Speak: Give a lecture at trade shows attended by prospective clients.
73.6   Speak: Speak somewhere to someone on your topic of expertise.
73.7   Speak: to an audience of potential clients.
73.8   Speak: Beef up resume by speaking at a local university.

74	Attend conferences.
75	Talk to the talkers.
76	Set up a speaking engagement with a well known celebrity or politician.
77.1	Teach: a class.
77.2	Teach: Conduct an evening course.
78	Support groups like Corstone.
79	Barter.
80.1	Sponsor: a charity's website.
80.2	Sponsor: or Co-sponsor a charitable event.
80.3	Sponsor: a bike race.
80.4	Sponsor: a children's school play whose parents are potential clients.
80.5	Sponsor: Girl Scouts, Boy Scouts, Cub Scouts, Life Scouts, Senior Scouts, etc.
81	Take an org poll amongst firm members.
82	Establish a "Markies" Night.
83	Have a "Findies" Award.
84.1	Get Political.
84.2	Get Political: Work with your local County or State U.S. Presidential Election Committee.
84.3	Get Political: Become a legal advisor to a politician.
84.4	Get Political: Become an advisor to a U.S. Senator in your State.
84.5	Get Political: Become an advisor to your U.S. Congressperson.
85	Run for an office.
86	Support your local District Attorney and State Attorney General.
87	In some obvious manner, support your local police and law enforcement agencies.
88	Send birthday cards to your clients, prospects and friends.
89	Fix a building.
90.1	Practice Area Research: Ask a Social Studies class to do a study on one of your practice areas.
90.2	Practice Area Research: Ask a University Masters, or PhD level, class to study the science and art of marketing professional legal services.
90.3	Practice Area Research: Test new practice areas.
91	Let a law student bring you business.
92.1	Tap university resources: Ask a university marketing class to adopt your law firm as a project.
92.2	Tap university resources: Ask a university advertising class to adopt your law firm as a project.
92.3	Tap university resources: Ask a University communications / public relations class to adopt your law firm as a project.
93	Think "cultural outreach."

94   Raise your SEO.

95.1   Web Power: Drive people to your website.

95.2   Web Power: Drive people to your website: Part Two.

95.3   Web Power: Use photos to drive even more people to your website, your virtual lobby.

95.4   Web Power: Add links on your website that would contribute to public service.

95.5   Web Power: Have a "Top 10" drop down button on your website.

95.6   Web Power: Create links on your website to government sites.

95.7   Web Power: Become a politician's new best friend.

95.8   Web Power: Drive politicians to your website.

95.9   Web Power: Add a Government Chart link to your website.

96.1   Web Charities: Create links on your site to charitable organizations.

96.2   Web Charities: Interview charity's Executive Director before adding their web link to your site.

97.1   Web Magnets: Create 100 reasons for people to come to your website.

97.2   Web Magnets: Add web links on your website that capture an even wider spectrum of online visitors.

97.3   Web Magnets: Add more web links on your website that capture an even wider spectrum of online visitors.

97.4   Web Magnets: Create 20 more reasons for people to come to your website.

97.5   Web Magnets: Inspire. Through the website offer a daily email with an inspiring quote.

98.1   FREE: Attract Prospects: Establish a website link titled www.MyFirmName.com/FREEStarbucksCard.

98.2   FREE: Trade Starbucks lattes for business leads.

99.1   `Web Magic: Have a Community Events Calendar link on your website.

99.2   Web Magic: Place a "must visit" Charitable Events Calendar link on the firm's website.

100   Twelve people who have to make me money.

Index

Acknowledgements

My inspiration comes from family, friends, role models, teachers, great writing, insightful media and life in its many manifestations, but most of all my passion and inspiration comes from my day to day companion, the love of my life, my wife.

About the Author

David King Keller is no stranger to the field of law, lawyers, and law firms.

His background includes: pre-law at the University of Maryland, founder of a publicly held corporation, Director and Trustee on multiple boards both for profit and 501C3, General Partner in real estate investments, landlord - lessor, commercial tenant - lessee, homeowner, civil rights advocate, inventor, commercial photographer, award winning film producer, writer, artist, sub-contractor on many advertising, marketing and PR campaigns, journalist, world traveler to 32 countries, day trader, motor vehicle accident victim, co-founding trustee of the San Francisco High School for Business and Commerce, Trustee of the California Institute of Integral Studies graduate school, recipient of multiple US Government security clearances, TV commercial writer-director, distributor of a food product into national chains, plaintiff, defendant, national and international mortgage industry consultant, Certified Mortgage Banker, campaign director of a US Congressional campaign, holder of an MBA from Pepperdine University, certified negotiator/mediator, certified executive coach, certified Neurolinguistic Professional, representative of a Fortune 500 Corporation to Australia's largest bank, 76 credits toward a PhD in East-West Psychology, University of California extension instructor, radio and TV guest discussing real estate and consumer products, periodic employer of some of San Francisco's biggest law firms, holder of numerous trademarks, and much more.

These and other experiences have given David more than casual contact with various areas of law including:

Alternative Dispute Resolution (ADR), Commercial Law, Contract Law, Torts, Family Law, Property Law, Bankruptcy, Business Law, Charitable Organizations, Civil Rights, Closely Held Businesses, Confidentiality Agreements, Conflicts of Interest, Consumer Law, Contract Law, Copyright, Corporate Law, Corporate Governance, Dispute Resolution, Employment Law, Enforcement of Judgments, Estate and Trust, Estate Planning,

Financing, Food and Drug, Health Law, Individual and Corporate Tax, Intellectual Property, Landlord and Tenant, Leasing Real Property, Litigation, Mediation, Mergers/Acquisitions, Mortgage, Non-Profit Organizations, Partnership, Patent, Products Liability, Real Estate Law, Real Estate - Commercial, Real Estate - Tax, Real Property, Residential Real Estate, Sales of Goods and Services, Secured Transactions, Securities, State/Local Tax, Tax Exempt Associations, Trademark, Wills, and more.

David is uniquely qualified to speak, coach, train, and write on the subject of business development because of the wide array of professional, promotional and problem solving skills he acquired from his national and international experiences growing companies from the one man shop to a Fortune 100 Corporation.

David has over 30 years of helping people through his competence in selling, marketing, advertising, promotion, inventing solutions to solve problems and resolving issues resulting in enhanced quality and service while improving revenue.

To increase XEROX copier sales David invented an adjustable document handler which XEROX said would improve sales by $98 million a year. To create a market for a powdered drink mix in a single-serving-packet David invented an all natural isotonic balanced multi-vitamin drink mix that did not harden on the store shelves thus allowing placement in a national grocery chain. He helped develop a market for a new color conversion film technique which brought him a national award for a short film on American Indians called "Legend Days Are Over." Ask David about his work for American Zoetrope, the Francis Ford Coppola and George Lucas venture.

David's people skills were honed even more when he was paid to lead groups of people to 32 different Countries for Olson Travelworld.

David is a certified professional Executive Coach with multiple certifications in coaching, counseling, consulting, mediation and negotiation.

While David was pre-law at the University of Maryland, his passion to help people called him to work with Martin Luther King's Poor People's Campaign. He took nurse's assistant training to assist folks who dared to live in Resurrection City on the Washington Mall. This led to his work as international co-director of Operation Outrage set up to feed the starving children in Biafra, Southern Nigeria. Following that, David worked as a subcontractor with numerous sales, marketing, publication relations, and advertising firms including J Walter Thompson. David's business development coaching benefits from his four years with XEROX sales and his training in XEROX' world famous programs: Professional Selling Skills and Need Satisfaction Selling. Since then David has spent years studying human behavior modes based on brain research, neurolinguistic programming and neuroscience research.

◇◇

David King Keller comes by his knowledge from many teachers and much experience.

A few photos follow with more on the book's website which provide examples of some of the Ways listed in the book such as marketing yourself to the media, creating TV ads, meeting key power brokers and the "A" list around them, and expanding one's credentials.

David Keller (in the middle) being
interviewed on KGO-TV's AM show.

David King Keller addressing UC Hastings College of The Law
alumni and 3Ls on the subject of law firm business development
with co-panelists (L to R) attorneys Jan Siok and Elena
DuCharme along with moderator, Sari Zimmerman,
Director, Office of Career & Professional Development.

David Keller with
President Jimmy Carter

David Keller was director of this TV Commercial
with NBA basketball star Nate Thurmond.

David Keller (on R) with now Senator Feinstein

David Keller (on L) discussing legislative ideas
with U.S. Senator Alan Cranston.

How to contact the author

DAVID KING KELLER
Keller Business Development Advisory Group
145 Corte Madera Town Center #520
Corte Madera, CA 94925
www.kbdag.com
David@100WaysToGrowAThrivingLawPractice.com
david@kbdag.com